Disabled Church –
Disabled Society

of related interest

From Isolation to Intimacy
Making Friends without Words
Phoebe Caldwell
With Jane Horwood
ISBN 978 1 84310 500 8

Promoting Social Interaction for Individuals with Communicative Impairments
Making Contact
Edited by M. Suzanne Zeedyk
ISBN 978 1 84310 539 8

Can the World Afford Autism Spectrum Disorder?
Nonverbal Communication, Asperger Syndrome and the Interbrain
Digby Tantam
ISBN 978 1 84310 694 4

Understanding Intensive Interaction
Context and Concepts for Professionals and Families
Graham Firth, Ruth Berry and Cath Irvine
ISBN 978 1 84310 982 2

Disabled Church – Disabled Society

THE IMPLICATIONS OF AUTISM FOR PHILOSOPHY, THEOLOGY AND POLITICS

JOHN GILLIBRAND

Foreword by Dr Rowan Williams

Afterword by Professor Anthony Bailey

Jessica Kingsley Publishers
London and Philadelphia

First published in 2010
by Jessica Kingsley Publishers
116 Pentonville Road
London N1 9JB, UK
and
400 Market Street, Suite 400
Philadelphia, PA 19106, USA

www.jkp.com

Library of Congress Cataloging in Publication Data
A CIP catalog record for this book is available from the Library of Congress

British Library Cataloguing in Publication Data
A CIP catalogue record for this book is available from the British Library

ISBN 978 1 84310 968 6

Printed and bound in Great Britain by
MPG Books Limited, Cornwall

To Gillian

who bore the burden and the heat of the day

Charity [Love] is the power to accept, to accept ourselves and other people and the world as the presence of God. Charity is the power not to deny but to affirm experience, not to shrink away from it in frozen or indignant alarm but to go out and meet it, because, in spite of the apparent threats and dangers, it is our creator, come not to steal, not to kill, not to destroy, but that we might have life, and have it more abundantly.

– Harry Williams (from *The True Wilderness –
A Selection of Addresses*, Constable, 1965)

What is the point of striving after knowledge if it only ensures the acquisition of knowledge and not in a certain way, and to the greatest extent possible, the disorientation of he who knows? What is philosophy today – I mean philosophical activity – if not the critical work of thought upon thought, if it does not, rather than legitimising what one already knows, consist of an attempt to know how, and to what extent it is possible to think differently.

– Michel Foucault (from the introduction to
The Use of Pleasures, Gallimard, 1984)

Autism is a disorder which fascinates because it seems to be so essentially a disorder of the human condition.

– Francesca Happé (*Autism – An Introduction to
Psychological Theory*, UCL Press, 1994)

Contents

Foreword

This is a book about living at the edge of what makes sense. It is first and foremost a book about the experience of living in a situation that doesn't submit to the 'ordinary' expectations of what can be managed and understood – the situation of parenting a child at the most challenging place in the autistic spectrum, with all the cost and stress this entails and all hard learning it brings. But it opens out from this into a wider reflection on making sense and failing to make sense. John Gillibrand observes with exceptional and uncomfortable clarity how much of our language about human dignity and human value still carries a coded assumption about what a human being 'really' is, and how heavy the strain ought to be on such language when we are engaged with a person who simply does not relate in the ways we commonly think about as standard. What if we are involved with a person who does not and cannot use language to define himself or herself? with a person who can't be said to be responding to emotional stimuli in any ways we can recognize? with a person who cannot with any credibility be said to be defined by conscious relations within a community? What is the appropriate response as we try to think of what is due to such a person in terms of rights and entitlements?

In the course of raising these questions, John directs some sharp challenges to both political and religious rhetoric. He is claiming, I think, that refusing to accept our failure to make sense is what most damages our thinking and feeling about people like his son, Adam. Theologically and socially, we want to 'contain' this threatening experience, to reduce people living with autism to problems to be managed; and so much of the language of the Church which John serves faithfully as a priest seems to take for granted things about relationship and community and speech that simply don't apply to his son, so that there is a constant, unspoken conspiracy of exclusion. What is powerful in these pages is that he does not offer a programme of rival solutions but only the invitation to let yourself be silenced by the puzzles and imaginative or intellectual brick walls that are recognized here.

But this is not a recommendation of passivity. The anger in this book is not only about religious insensitivity or social nervousness and avoidance. It is very profoundly about the loss of political nerve in a cultural climate that has made the whole enterprise of *care* so marginal to its concerns, and now seems unable to accept that it has come to the end of its resources in terms of capacity to 'fix' things, economically, socially and environmentally. The imperative to address the priority of care afresh with proper seriousness just might be felt more acutely in this situation of losing the power to make sense in the ways we once took for granted – so that this just might turn out to be a moment of grace after all. And at the most fundamental level of all, the summons is to let go of the patronizing downward look at those who are different; John is not afraid of making the connection between attitudes to autism and the Church's confusion and fear around sexual minorities. The 'sense', the meaning, that matters is ultimately made when we acknowledge that the other's situation is our own, that there is no tidy frontier between the world in which we are in charge as makers of sense and the world of those poor unfortunates who can't make sense or make the wrong kind of sense. 'In *them*, it is *us* that we all see', he writes; we are all faced with senselessness, and we find a properly human meaning when we face that truth before the unnameable God and the 'failed' and crucified saviour.

Combining poignant personal honesty with an extraordinarily wide range of theological and philosophical learning, John Gillibrand has written a book that takes us well beyond the usual boundaries of studies in autism to raise questions about our human identity, suggesting that we jeopardize human dignity most when we try to bind it to the characteristics we can recognize and value and understand as mirroring only our own faces. The harder labour is seeing ourselves in the person who is genuinely and painfully other; and this is what John and Gill have seen as their calling in discovering how to be parents to Adam. I am grateful that they have shared with us what this calling means through these searching and moving pages.

Dr Rowan Williams
Archbishop of Canterbury
Lambeth Palace
January 2010

Acknowledgements

I have already expressed my thanks to my wife Gillian in the dedication. I also thank my parents, Dr. Maurice Gillibrand and Mary Gillibrand, for all the support which they have given down the years. My father is an agnostic; my mother is an Anglican. Putting the two together, all the time, produces a book like this. My other son, Peter, has been a tower of strength. I am constantly renewed and refreshed by talking with him, and sharing in learning. As this book was being written he visited Disneyland in Paris. In the motorway services on the way home he became anxiously aware that he had not purchased presents for his parents. With the money he had left, he purchased two books for the price of one. For me, he brought home Dawkins' *The God Delusion.*

Sadly, some time before the writing of this book, Adam and Peter's other grandparents, Jack and Alma Lewis, had died. They too gave us endless support and were with us the night we arrived home after Adam's diagnosis. Alma always used to tell her friends in the Ladies' Guild at St. Mary's Croesyceiliog about Adam. They would always ask her about him, knowing how proud she and Jack were of their first grandchild.

Over the years, I have incurred many and various intellectual debts. It has always been my ambition that my son Adam should have whatever is for him an education of equivalent quality to the one that I have received. Any virtues in this book far more reflect the capacity of my teachers than my own. It is good to be able to do what Adam will never have the opportunity to do, which is to say thank you.

Among many others, I would like to give especial thanks to the following. The late Father Eric Franklin was my tutor in New Testament at St. Stephen's House, Oxford. He spent Millennium Eve with us as a family, at a moment in history when most people did not want to be faced so directly with the issues of caring for a person with autism. His constant advice to his students in regard to the New Testament was to 'get it in your guts'. He realized that there is far more to New Testament studies than the pure intellectual response: it has to be made applicable to the gut reality of human life.

The Rev'd Dr. John Heywood-Thomas was the supervisor of my University of Wales PhD thesis. It was written while working as a parish priest and caring for a teenager with autism. Many times I would have given up. Because of his (almost) infinite patience I persevered, and now I am glad that I did.

Archbishop Rowan Williams was the external examiner for my University of Wales doctorate on *The Applicability of the Thought of Michel Foucault to Christian Theology*. He will be aware how much the thought of Foucault stands behind much of what has been written here. I am most grateful that he encouraged me to turn the original short essay on which all this is based into a book, at a time when, for reasons which will become obvious, I was uncertain that I could or indeed should do so.

Dr. Ross McKibbin, Emeritus Research Fellow at St. John's College, Oxford, almost 30 years ago taught me nineteenth- and twentieth-century history, at a time when my chief concern was with discovering the heritage of Victorian religion. He set me an undergraduate essay on the secularization of Victorian society. I do not know what he said in the subsequent tutorial, but it is a topic on which I have been reflecting ever since, with consequences (I hope fruitful) which appear in these pages.

Dr. Malcolm Vale, also a fellow at St. John's, is a medievalist. As a theologian, one is often forced to concern oneself with the Reformation, the Scientific Revolution, the Enlightenment, modernity and postmodernity. It is good to be able to view those things not just from after, but from before. Malcolm has helped me to have some access to that colourful world, to be able to imagine a world that is otherwise.

Over 20 years ago, I began to learn Welsh in order to exercise a priestly ministry in Welsh-speaking Wales. I would gladly give one of my two languages to my non-lingual son, if he wanted it. Lord Dafydd Elis-Thomas has helped me to set language acquisition in its social and political context, to have begun to reflect, long before Adam came into the world, on what is text, and what is discourse.

The following very kindly reviewed my work at different stages in its development, and offered both support and critical comment: Dr. Medwin Hughes, Vice Chancellor of Trinity University College, Carmarthen; the Rev'd Dr. Alun Evans, formerly head of production at the BBC in Bangor, and former president of the court of the National Eisteddfod of Wales; Euryn Ogwen Williams, formerly deputy chief executive of S4C; Professor Gareth Crompton, sometime Chief Medical Officer for Wales; Chris Harvey, OBE, sometime headteacher of Hawarden High School; Trevor Nesirky, formerly director of Progress Care and Education; Philippa Nesirky, Residential Services Manager for Rehab Care, Ireland.

My day-to-day life is not lived within the academy. I want to express special thanks to my parishioners in the parishes of Llangeler with Penboyr, and to the people of the five churches of (in alphabetical order) St. Barnabas, St. Celer, St. James, St. Llawddog and Capel Mair. They, and the members of the wider community here, without perhaps realizing that they were doing it, so restored my faith in the church and in human nature in general. None of us ask more or less than to be accepted for who we are and as we are. Once we have asked that, we have asked for all that is necessary.

Thanks go finally to all those who have cared for Adam over what are now many long years. There are too many names to record here, but our special thanks go to those who are now looking after Adam at Rowden House; to Suzie Bateman and Krysztof Tokawski who have been in turn his key workers; to Helen Squire, Ruth Goddard, Sue Downey and Jackie Holloway who have been his class teachers, and to whoever is there for him and with him today.

Introduction –
Who is This Book For?

I am the father of Adam, a teenager on the autistic spectrum. This book is an attempt to reflect at the deeper level upon his life and the experience of caring for him. It will be immediately obvious that the experiences of caring which are described in this book would have been difficult for anybody. Those who, for whatever reason, have been through experiences of similar intensity will immediately recognize the geography of the place described. For those who, thank God, have not been through such things, welcome to this land, and please do not be deterred from pressing on beyond the border. I came to those experiences, and went through them with a certain set of beliefs and ways of thinking. I have been trained in philosophy and theology, and was therefore somewhat familiar with the riches of the Western tradition of thought. One by one, I found key points of that tradition held up to challenge by the simple experience of living with and desperately caring for a person with profound autism. Before I ever studied theology and philosophy, I read a degree in history, and was taught the value of analytic, rational, objective history. That training goes deep, and I am therefore more than a little sceptical of 'first person' accounts of anything. In any academic study, the simple use of the word 'I' can darken the way that leads to objective truth. Whether objective truth exists or not, one should not attempt to seek it on a road thus darkened. However, what you will find in this book is an account which moves, sometimes quite suddenly, from first person narrative to philosophical, theological and historical reflection upon that narrative. I have tried to keep those shifts to a minimum, and not to make them too extreme. However, given the project, they are inevitable. Both theology and philosophy are tempted to work within their own worlds and follow their own intellectual and other rituals. What I have attempted to do is to smash them up against the brute reality of day-to-day life, and then to see what remains.

I am a serving Anglican priest with the Church in Wales. I would like to think that this book will be of interest to those in ordained ministry in any of the Christian denominations, as well as those in positions of leadership in other faith communities. In the body of the text I use the term 'priest' to describe what I do and what I am: this is a reflection of the Anglican-Catholic tradition in which I received my theological formation. I hope that those who belong to other Christian traditions and indeed other faith communities will take from these reflections what they find useful. My aim is to be of assistance to those in a similar role to myself for whom reflective practice – comprising both theological and philosophical reflection – is of importance.

It is worth indicating where I would now locate myself on the spectrum of the Christian tradition. My early upbringing was with a traditionally minded low-church setting. During my adolescent and college years, I experienced the wealth of the Catholic tradition within Anglicanism, and it is from that experience that my calling to the priesthood arose. In 1987, while I was still at theological college, the General Synod of the Church of England passed a vote which began the progress towards the ordination of women to the priesthood in 1992. Seeing that controversy from so close at hand led me to a questioning of the Catholic tradition which had provided such spiritual nourishment. Within parish ministry, I have always sought to work closely with colleagues who belong to the Evangelical tradition within the Church: however, it is a tradition which I have not shared, and which I do not share. The experiences which I will describe with Adam sent me on a trajectory which on a cursory observation could be described as a movement towards a more liberal form of Anglican catholicism, continuing the process which had been accelerated at the time of my theological training. I do not however think that what will be found in these pages is adequately described by the label 'liberal christianity'. There are a number of reasons for thinking this. First and foremost 'liberal' has become a polemic term in all kinds of political and ecclesiastical contexts, and may therefore be coming to the end of any genuine usefulness. Second, while wishing to move the terms of the theological debate into new territory, in ways which we shall explore, and which will be made very explicit in the conclusion, I would strongly affirm that the material that I will be using to do that belongs to the mainstream of Christian orthodoxy. About that, the reader will have to make up her or his own mind. However, I would like to think that there are far more interesting questions arising from these pages than 'Is John Gillibrand an orthodox Anglican or not?'

Thus, we have here the thought that we are dealing with the contemporary context of Anglican parish ministry, as undertaken by reflective practitioners. It will be suggested that there is an impasse within that contemporary context, which, without any further description at this stage, may well be familiar to those in ordained ministry who are reading this. I have reason to believe that theological and philosophical reflection upon the very specific personal circumstances of caring for a child at the extreme end of the autistic spectrum may well have suggested some ways for us all to move beyond that impasse. It should be stressed that I offer the thoughts within this volume with a degree of humility. Like all parish clergy, I have strengths and weaknesses. I sometimes get things right. I have sometimes made errors of judgement. I should imagine that all parish clergy share my frustration that those who see the clerical collar are strangely prevented from seeing the humanity of the person who wears it. This book arises not from a sense that I have some unique perception of the solutions, but from a particular way of viewing the problems, a certain angle.

Beyond my own professional peers, this book will be of interest to those who, from outside the church, find the church interesting, as a sociological, organizational and economic phenomenon. One should caution that my own experience, first as a carer and second as one most of whose time as a priest has been spent in rural contexts, is scarcely typical of most parish clergy. However, in the process of imagining the direction in which the Anglican Church could go, I will be describing – from an insider's perspective – our starting point, the way things are for clergy and congregations today. The tools of analysis, because of my own background, will be conjointly theological and philosophical, without giving priority to either, without allowing the one to destroy the integrity of the other. It would therefore be possible – this is certainly the intention – for someone whose reflective practice is rooted in philosophy rather than theology to read this with benefit.

I can no longer believe, for reasons which I hope will become apparent, that there is a hard line of division between the sacred and the secular, mirrored in the relationship between theology and philosophy. I do believe that the Church's engagement with the world calls Christians to political action, and I would root such action within the stand of liberation theology. I will explore what it could mean for a disabled person to experience liberation, and the kind of political agenda which a liberation theology would set. I would therefore like to think that what is written here will be of interest both to those who are engaged in the political process and to those who find themselves marginalized by it.

This book is intended for a special group of people who often find themselves on the margins both of the political process and of church life: the parents and carers of those on the autistic spectrum or with Asperger Syndrome. There is only one thing that I have found more difficult than responding to what I believe was a call to the priesthood, and that is sharing in the care of a child at the extreme end of the autistic spectrum. Whatever view of the world which one has at the point of diagnosis, whatever theology or ideology one espouses, it will over subsequent years be subject to enormous challenges. Thus, I hope that this book will help those who are impelled by any kind of experience of care to reflect on questions of deeper meaning. What is written here is specific to autism, but all of those engaged in the daily task of caring will recognize something of their own lives.

Those on the autistic spectrum with expressive language often express profound frustration, and indeed annoyance, with the attitudes of parents and carers, and indeed the attitudes of our wider society. Society – whatever that may be – treats autism as a problem to be managed or 'solved', rather than seeing the actual people with autism, and recognizing their full citizenship within the State. I would hope that this book, alongside the enormous efforts of many others, contributes in some way to the raising of autism awareness. The National

Autistic Society at the time of writing is running a campaign 'I exist': it would seem that God and people with autism share a similar problem of convincing others of their existence.

I am aware that the task outlined here is vast in scope. I would suggest that Adam, all but voiceless, very needy, powerless according to the usual standards of this world, may well have much to teach us.

Terminology – The Use of Words

Autism as a lifelong development disorder is classified as a learning disability. On occasions in the text, I also refer to autism as a cognitive disability. I include those with autism among those who have cognitive deficits. There are those who otherwise can be described as having learning difficulties, but autism does not belong to that category. A cognitively 'able' person may well have cognitive deficits which arise from being cognitively able. I talk later on about the problems which categorization and the associated labelling bring with them.

I am careful about the use of gender-inclusive language, as I believe this to be part of a wider agenda of inclusion. Where non-inclusive language appears it is only because I am reproducing the words of the original source.

There is a whole range of language about disabilities which reveals the unspoken assumptions of the society which utters that language. I do not regard autism as an 'affliction' from which people 'suffer'. Such terminology medicalizes autism, and indeed disability in general: autism is not a disease. To refuse to medicalize autism is not to deny its existence: I prefer to speak of people 'with autism'. I have beyond this some sympathy with the view expressed by Olga Bogdashina in her work on *Sensory and Perceptual Issues in Autism and Asperger Syndrome*:

> I deliberately use the term 'autistic people' rather than 'people with autism' because autism is not something that is just attached to them and cannot be easily removed. I am aware of the 'people first, then disability' approach. However without autism they would be different people, as being autistic means being different. If people with autism prefer to name themselves autistic why should we be

One Perspective

shy to call them that? Just to show them our respect? There are other ways to do it. Autism is not something to be ashamed of.[1]

For good reasons, people with autism are sometimes said to have 'autistic spectrum disorders'. The word 'disorder' allows us to escape from other terminology, the terminology of retardation and handicap, and it is therefore retained here. Beautifully, in the United States, section 2.A.2 of the Combating Autism Act of 2006 amends the Public Health Service Act 'by striking the term "autism" each place such term appears [...] and inserting "autism spectrum disorder"'. However, as will be seen, I am not sure that we can regard those with autism as fundamentally 'disordered': to do so would be to presume that we know what an ordered life is, and I do not believe that we have that knowledge. Equally, the concept of a 'spectrum' can allow for too much flexibility in the provision of public services for people with autism, as almost 'theological' distinctions are made as to where a particular person is located on the spectrum.

Issue 1

Issue 2

---

1   Bogdashina (2003), p. 19.

CHAPTER 1

What is Autism?

I am not going to seek in this chapter to cover territory that is far better done in other books, but simply to provide enough background information to assist in the understanding of what follows. The word *autistic* was first used by Eugen Bleuler, in a 1912 edition of the *American Journal of Insanity*. The concern of his article was in the first place to describe the social withdrawal associated with schizophrenia.[1] The word is derived from the Greek word for self *autos*. Much of the modern thinking about autism is traced back to Leo Kanner's seminal paper in 1943, *'Autistic disturbances of affective contact'*.[2] Kanner's paper was quickly followed in 1944 by the work of Hans Asperger, which gave rise to the term Asperger Syndrome.[3] It is deeply ironic that at the time of the Second World War, when the peoples of the world were so disastrously failing to communicate with each other, Kanner and Asperger should be investigating the lives of those whose challenges so much revolve around difficulties of communication and social contact. Indeed, the school which Asperger founded in his native Austria for young people with autism was bombed in the closing stages of the war.

The diagnosis of autism has all kinds of issues attached to it. As Aarons and Gittens point out, 'Problems relating to the diagnosis of autism have been apparent ever since Kanner's time. The situation

---

1   Happé (1994), p. 107.
2   *Nervous Child*, 2, pp. 217–250.
3   'Die "Autistischen Psychopathen" im Kindesalter' *Archiv für Psychiatrie und Nervenkrankheiten*, 117, pp. 76–136.

remains far from satisfactory and remains fraught with muddle and confusion.'[4] In section 299.00 of the standard diagnostic manual the Diagnostic and Statistical Manual of Mental Disorders (DSM-IV),[5] published by the American Psychiatric Association, autism is defined as follows. It is done as a list.

1. A total of six (or more) items from (1), (2) and (3), with at least two from (1), and one each from (2) and (3):

(1) qualitative impairment in social interaction, as manifested by at least two of the following:
  1. marked impairment in the use of multiple non-verbal behaviours such as eye-to-eye gaze, facial expression, body postures, and gestures to regulate social interaction
  2. failure to develop peer relationships appropriate to developmental level
  3. a lack of spontaneous seeking to share enjoyment, interests, or achievements with other people (e.g. by a lack of showing, bringing, or pointing out objects of interest)
  4. lack of social or emotional reciprocity

(2) qualitative impairments in communication as manifested by at least one of the following:
  1. delay in, or total lack of, the development of spoken language (not accompanied by an attempt to compensate through alternative modes of communication such as gesture or mime)
  2. in individuals with adequate speech, marked impairment in the ability to initiate or sustain a conversation with others
  3. stereotyped and repetitive use of language or idiosyncratic language
  4. lack of varied, spontaneous make-believe play or social imitative play appropriate to developmental level

---

4   1992, p. 23. Chapter IV of the book 'Problems of diagnosis' gives an extended discussion of some of the causes of this 'muddle and confusion', and especially the vexed question as to the inclusion within the diagnosis of those who are presenting with 'autistic features'.

5   One could also refer to the World Health Organization's International Classification of Diseases (2007) version (ICD-10) which at F84 covers Pervasive Developmental Disorders, including childhood autism (F84.0), atypical autism (F84.1), Asperger's syndrome (F84.5). http://www.who.int/classifications/apps/icd/icd10online/ [accessed 26th May 2008].

(3) restricted repetitive and stereotyped patterns of behaviour, interests, and activities, as manifested by at least one of the following:

    1. encompassing preoccupation with one or more stereotyped and restricted patterns of interest that is abnormal either in intensity or focus

    2. apparently inflexible adherence to specific, nonfunctional routines or rituals

    3. stereotyped and repetitive motor mannerisms (e.g. hand or finger flapping or twisting, or complex whole-body movements)

    4. persistent preoccupation with parts of objects

2. Delays or abnormal functioning in at least one of the following areas, with onset prior to age 3 years:

(1) social interaction

(2) language as used in social communication

(3) symbolic or imaginative play.

3. The disturbance is not better accounted for by Rett's Disorder or Childhood Disintegrative Disorder.

In brief, the only one of these items which is not applicable to Adam is 1.2(2), and this only because he is not an individual who has developed 'adequate' speech.

The actual number of people with autism has been controversial. There are many who have talked of an autism epidemic. One campaigner who has used this term repeatedly is Congressman Dan Burton, a member of the US House of Representatives, who speaks of 'this literal epidemic' of autism.[6] In the United States the Centers for Disease Control and Prevention (CDC) have an Autism and Developmental Disabilities Monitoring (ADDM) Network. In February 2007, the CDC issued a prevalence survey from this network, which claimed to be 'the first and largest summary of prevalence data from multiple US communities participating in an autism spectrum disorder (ASD) surveillance project'.[7] The ADDM sampled a range of communities from

---

6   Congressional Record, February 2006. http://burton.house.gov/posts/burton-calls-for-a-white-house-conference-on-autism [accessed 15 December 2010].

7   http://www.cdc.gov/media/pressrel/2007/r070208.htm?s_cid=mediarel_r070208 [accessed 18 August 2009].

different states across the USA. The finding was that an average of 6.7 children out of 1000 had an ASD in the six communities assessed in 2000, and an average of 6.6 children out of 1000 had an ASD in the 14 communities included in the 2002 study. This finding translates to approximately one in 150 children in these communities. As the CDC pointed out: 'for decades, the best estimate for the prevalence of autism was four to five per 10,000 children'. The conclusions of the CDC are reflected by research in the United Kingdom. In July 2006, Professor Gillian Baird and others published findings in *The Lancet* under the title: 'Prevalence of disorders of the autism spectrum in a population cohort of children in South Thames: the Special Needs and Autism Project (SNAP)'. This used a large total sample of 56,946 children between the ages of nine and ten. Their conclusion was that the 'prevalence of autism and related ASDs is substantially greater than previously recognized'. Within their sample 'the total prevalence of all ASDs' was 116.1 per 10,000.[8] Estimating prevalence of ASDs within the adult population is more difficult. Although there are cases in which a full diagnosis is only made at some stage in adulthood, children with autism tend to be known to the local educational services and to some extent to social services. In February 2008, a *Postnote* on the subject of autism for the Parliamentary Office of Science and Technology acknowledged that 'there has been no robust survey of the number of autistic adults'.[9] As a result of this gap in knowledge, on 8 May 2008, the United Kingdom health minister Ivan Lewis announced £500,000 of funding for a project to calculate the total number of adults with autism in England.

The apparent increase in autism has generated a widespread debate about what causes autism. Some are prepared to put the increased prevalence down to more sophisticated techniques of diagnosis, and greater public awareness. Factors which are often considered are the dietary and the environmental. The sharp controversy about the role of the

---

8   Within the statistical range of 90.4–141.8. Gillian Baird, Emily Simonoff, Andrew Pickles, Susie Chandler, Tom Loucas, David Meldrum, Tony Charman (2006) 'Prevalence of disorders of the autism spectrum in a population cohort of children in South Thames: the Special Needs and Autism Project (SNAP)', *The Lancet* 368 (9531), 15 July, pp.210–215.

9   Postnote, no. 302, 'Autism'. This can be consulted at http://www.parliament.uk/documents/upload/postpn302.pdf [accessed 19 May 2008].

MMR[10] vaccine was, as is well known, triggered by Andrew Wa
original article in *The Lancet*.[11] These controversies highlight the neeu
for government investment and research. As things stand at the time
of writing, autism remains in many ways mysterious: we do not know
what causes autism, or indeed whether there is one single cause. It may
well be that there are predisposing factors, and a number of triggers
which are effective if the predisposing factors are present.

I am not going to attempt to give an exhaustive account of all
the theories regarding the causation of autism, but would rather like
to highlight two particular areas of research which will have specific
relevance for this book.

One particular theory which has attracted a lot of attention is
that children with autism do not develop a 'theory of mind'. In 1993,
Oxford University Press published a substantial and technical collection of essays on this subject *Understanding Other Minds*, edited by
Simon Baron-Cohen, Helen Tager-Flusberg and Donald Cohen. The
introduction described the theory at the heart of the debate:

> It is known as the *theory of mind hypothesis of* autism. By 'theory of
> mind' is meant the ability of normal children to attribute mental
> states (such as beliefs, desires, intentions etc.) to themselves and
> other people, as a way of making sense of and predicting behav-
> iour. The theory of mind hypothesis of autism holds that in chil-
> dren with autism, this ability fails to develop in the normal way,
> resulting in the observed social and communication abnormalities
> in behaviour.[12]

In a subsequent extended essay *Mindblindness*, Simon Baron-Cohen
seeks to describe this way of being from within, in other words he
seeks imaginatively to recreate the mental state of another person in
ways which a person with 'mindblindness' would find beyond their
repertoire. 'Imagine', says Baron-Cohen:

> what your world would be like if you were aware of physical things
> but were blind to the existence of mental things. I mean, of course,

---

10   Measles, mumps and rubella.
11   Wakefield A.J., Murch S.H., Anthony A., *et al.* (1998) 'Ileal-lymphoid-nodular
      hyperplasia, non-specific colitis, and pervasive developmental disorder in children',
      Lancet 351 (9103), pp.637–41.
12   Baron-Cohen *et al.* (1993), p. 3.

blind to things like thoughts, beliefs, knowledge, desires, and intentions, which for most of us self evidently underlie behaviour. Stretch your imagination to consider what sense you could make of human action (or, for that matter, any animate action whatsoever) if, as for a behaviourist, a mentalistic explanation was forever beyond your limits. This is a hard thought experiment.[13]

Without wishing to anticipate many arguments to which I shall later turn, 'thoughts, beliefs, knowledge, desires and intentions' are the basic common working material of theologians and philosophers.

Much investigation has also been given to the question of a genetic causation for autism. As Uta Frith points out, 'Scientists have long suspected a genetic basis.'[14] She continues by summarizing the state of research in this area as it stood in 2003:

Having established a genetic basis for autism, the search for the location of potentially predisposing genes has become a fast moving area of research. It has proved to be very difficult however. This is partly because nobody knows what genes to look for, and partly because the current diagnostic procedures might actually fail to make the most appropriate classification. Large families with several affected members are rare, but it is these families that allow a particularly promising genetic approach. Here the chromosomes of both affected and unaffected relatives are screened and compared in minute detail. As yet no consistent story has emerged from this work.[15]

Thus the mystery remains. Frith suggests that this mysteriousness may be easier for scientists to handle than parents:

Scientists are skeptical of the abundant suggestions of physical and chemical causes of autism that are constantly being produced. They can live with the abstract idea that the causes of autism are not yet known. Parents find this much more difficult. When no explanation is given of why their healthy and beautiful baby has autism, they are compelled to search for a cause.[16]

---

13 Baron-Cohen (1995), p. 1.
14 Frith (2003), p. 70. She cites Michael Rutter's article of 2000 in the *American Journal of Psychiatry*, 18, 297–321: 'Genetic studies of autism: From the 1970s into the millenium.'
15 Ibid., p. 71.
16 Ibid., p. 75.

In the course of this book, we will return to the theme of the mysteriousness of autism, and how to respond to the mystery.

Less mysterious is the vast cost of autism. The care of people with autism costs an enormous amount of money, and autism has considerable economic impacts. In 2007, Martin Knapp, Renée Romeo, and Jennifer Beacham, working at the Centre for the Economics of Mental Health, in the Institute of Psychiatry at King's College London, with advice from the Foundation for People with Learning Disabilities, produced the study *The Economic Consequences of Autism in the UK*. This built on their earlier work. The headline figures from the executive summary are striking:

> **Total annual UK costs** We multiplied [...] individual-level costs by estimates of prevalence rates, distinguishing type of accommodation, level of functioning and age group. The aggregate national costs of supporting children with ASD were estimated to be £2.7 billion each year. Most of this cost is accounted for by services used. For adults, the aggregate costs for adults amount to £25 billion each year. Of this total, 59% is accounted for by services, 36% by lost employment for the individual with ASD, and the remainder by family expenses.[17]

When we meet a person with autism, there is more to them than their label, or their diagnosis. There is also more to them than the puzzle of what makes them the way they are. There is definitely more to them than the price tag which society places on the way they are. We need to see beyond that to individuality and difference. As we have seen above, following the work of the English psychiatrist Dr. Lorna Wing, autism is now commonly seen as a spectrum disorder.[18] This makes allowance for individuality and difference. What is true of all of us, is true of people with autism, that each is individual. In the next chapter, I will give us a fuller opportunity to meet an individual with autism.

---

17   Knapp *et al.* (2007), p. 2. Available to download at http://www.learningdisabilities.
      org.uk/publications/?EntryId5=28948&char=E [accessed 15 September 2008].

18   See Wing (1996) and above, p. 24.

CHAPTER 2

Adam, A Biography

Biography is usually reserved for the older and the famous, those who are considered to have achieved something, such as a great actor, speaker, or politician. In one way, those with disabilities do not appear in history. They are not the agents of historical change. In another way, especially in the records of institutions, they leave more historical trace than others would.[1] Some biographies are more intrusive than others. I will here seek to give an honest, difficult account of the reality of our life, while safeguarding the privacy of Adam, and ourselves as his family. The living subjects of biographies sometimes disagree with what is written about them. I am mindful that Adam cannot disagree or agree, and it is worth recording that – in ways that may in the nature of things not be immediately apparent – I have been highly sensitive to this. In this chapter, I am also describing an individual caught within the legal structures and bureaucracy of the educational, health and social care systems. I will seek to highlight the associated issues in the order in which they presented themselves to us as a family.

Gillian and I were married in February 1992. Gill had been a primary school teacher in the South Wales valleys. I was from Manchester, had learnt Welsh, and had just been appointed as the Rector of the Parish of Ffestiniog, a slate mining community in the heart of the North Welsh countryside. Adam was born on 4 June 1993. The doctor came into the delivery room, examined him and told us he was fine. We took him back from Ysbyty Gwynedd, the hospital in Bangor, to

---

1   See below, p. 156

Blaenau Ffestiniog. I remember bringing his Moses basket into the house, and thinking – probably like any new father – that this would change everything. His name in Hebrew, in the book of Genesis, besides being the personal name of the 'first man', can also be taken as a generic term for humanity. Adam has never fully responded to his personal name.

    In his earliest years, our main concern was that it was a long time before he started walking. To go from place to place he used to lie on his back and push himself with his legs in a kind of swimming motion. It was this delay in walking which first brought him to the attention of the health visitors. In his earliest years we were aware that Adam was different. The Checklist for Autism in Toddlers (CHAT), intended to be taken as part of the 18-month developmental test, asks the following questions of parents, with the highlighted words as in the original:

1. Does your child enjoy being swung, bounced on your knee, etc.? yes

2. Does your child take an interest in other children? yes (then)

3. Does your child like climbing on things, such as up stairs? yes

4. Does your child enjoy playing peek-a-boo/hide-and-seek? yes

5. Does your child ever PRETEND, for example, to make a cup of tea using a toy cup and teapot, or pretend other things? yes (then)

6. Does your child ever use his/her index finger to point, to ASK for something? (yes, then)

7. Does your child ever use his/her index finger to point, to indicate INTEREST in something? (yes, then)

8. Can your child play properly with small toys (e.g. cars or bricks) without just mouthing, fiddling or dropping them? (yes, then)

9. Does your child ever bring objects over to you (parent) to SHOW you something? (yes, then)

At the same time, the general practitioner or health visitor is invited to make these observations, in confirmation of the parental answers.

1. During the appointment, has the child made eye contact with you?

2. Get child's attention, then point across the room at an interesting object and say 'Oh look! There's a (name of toy!)' Watch child's face. Does the child look across to see what you are pointing at?

3. Get the child's attention, then give child a miniature toy cup and teapot and say 'Can you make a cup of tea?' Does the child pretend to pour out tea, drink it, etc.?

4. Say to the child 'Where's the light?', or 'Show me the light'. Does the child point with his/her index finger at the light?

5. Can the child build a tower of bricks? (If so, how many?)[2]

Gillian remembers that Adam would enjoy being bounced on her knee, and could – though not without fail – construct a tower of blocks. The answer to all these questions would otherwise be a negative, and that would still be the same answer today. At the time, I suspect that we were in denial, not wanting to believe that our child was developing other than on the lines of what some call 'normal'. In his nineteenth month, Adam, much to our relief, hauled himself to his feet and walked, but by then the other challenges were becoming increasingly apparent. Most notably, Adam did not begin to develop speech, and did not seem to make eye contact. He looked above and beyond and around us. Early parenthood is in many ways a time of enchantment; for us some of those first, shared experiences simply went missing. At this early stage, a meeting of professionals concerned with Adam's care was convened. It was suggested that Adam would be likely to need a statement of special educational needs. As parents we embraced this idea with enthusiasm, being – albeit dimly – aware that a statement would bring with it a legal entitlement to additional educational support. Adam began to attend on a part-time basis the pre-school assessment unit attached to our local primary school, Ysgol Maenofferen.

---

2   The details are to be found on the National Autistic Society's website: http://www. nas.org.uk/nas/jsp/polopoly.jsp?d=128&a=2226 [accessed 26 May 2008].

In 1997 we moved to Menai Bridge, partly to be nearer the support of my parents, and partly because we were by then aware that Adam might well need to attend a special school, which would have been located either on Anglesey (Ysgol y Bont), or in Caernarfon (Ysgol Pendalar). At this stage, Adam had not yet received a diagnosis. As a key local expert was away on maternity leave, we were referred to the Early Years Diagnostic Centre in Nottingham. A few weeks before, I had been listening to the historian Norman Stone on *Desert Island Discs* describing to Sue Lawley the difficulties which he had encountered in caring for his daughter who is on the autistic spectrum. I found the programme interesting, because of my knowledge of Adam, but I did not make the specific connection to autism.

Thus, in October at the end of 1997, we made our way to Nottingham, to the Early Years Diagnostic Centre, which in 2004 was renamed the Elizabeth Newson Centre. We were seen there by the Director of the Centre, Dr. Phil Christie, a consultant child psychologist. The centre's website still describes the play-based assessment that took place:

> The diagnostic assessment is based on observation and analysis of a total of three hours' structured and unstructured play with the child. Two hours of this takes place in a specially equipped playroom, and will be observed by parents and staff together through a large one-way screen; parents and child have as much access to each other as is needed to keep the child happy. During this time, we also take a comprehensive past and present history. During the third hour, in fine weather the child is also observed in our adventure playground, or in and around the centre and attached nursery and infants school if wet. After a short break, parents and staff use this third hour to discuss some of our conclusions.[3]

I remember the place as open, airy, and friendly. I remember the anxiety of looking through the screen and worrying what Adam might do, and how these people with their expert knowledge would respond to that; what these unfamiliar people might be thinking, of us, and of Adam. Gill and I were afraid because Adam's future was unknown. If we had known the future – the future implications of that diagnosis day – it would have been too much to bear. After a few hours, we had

---

3   http://www.sutherlandhouse.org.uk/ [accessed 26 May 2008].

the opportunity to discuss matters with Dr. Christie. There is a God-given skill to breaking difficult news, and I remember that everything was done with extreme and professional sensitivity. The experience of parents at the point of diagnosis is not always of this quality.[4] The message was that Dr. Christie believed Adam to be on the autistic spectrum, and that we would, over the next few weeks, receive a full report on him. Gill cried, rather quietly. I put my arm round her. I remember a wanting to be elsewhere, trying to reassure the staff that we were ready to make our way to the local hotel, though I was dreading managing Adam's behaviour in a strange environment. We got to the car. The car would not start. About six or seven hours later the recovery lorry got us back to Menai Bridge, where Gill's parents had been looking after Adam's baby brother Peter. It was only then that I rested my head down upon my folded arms, broke down, and wept.

Parents and carers face more than one difficulty: there is the practical task of caring for a person with autism and, while caring, coming to terms with that autism. However much, for Adam's sake, we want it to be otherwise, there is always the awareness of the might-have-beens, especially as Adam hits the different age milestones of what is called 'normal' development. Beyond these challenges, the day of diagnosis marks the beginning for so many families of what is an unending struggle to secure appropriate public services, both for the member of the family and for themselves as carers.

I will return later to our household life. The first major challenge following the diagnosis was to do with Adam's education. We have never imagined that it was suitable for Adam to be educated in the mainstream, and he therefore began his full-time education at a special school, Ysgol y Bont in Llangefni. We always felt enormous warmth and support from the school community. Adam began in the reception class, in a group of pupils with a range of disabilities. Adam's statement of special educational needs was intended to specify where he would receive his education, and the nature of the provision that would be made for him in the light of his needs. I was by then aware that it was necessary to get the text of the statement absolutely correct since its contents were, and are, legally enforceable. I was also aware of the professional view that early intervention is highly beneficial in

---

4   See Osbourne and Reed (2008).

the outcomes for people with autism, and of the benefits to Adam of highly individualized attention. Thus the negotiation between ourselves and the local education authority (LEA) hinged around whether the statement should include the words 'a highly favourable child adult ratio' or 'a 2–1 child adult ratio'. I was concerned that unless the latter phraseology was used, we would not be able adequately to defend Adam's best interests in the future. Given the other pressures upon us as family, I did not want to have to renegotiate his provision whenever there was a shift in the overall needs of the population of the school which he happened to attend. The dual role of the educational psychologist within the statementing process, with responsibility for clinical assessment as well as acting as one of the gatekeepers of the local education authority's special needs budget, has already been highlighted in public debate.[5] Apart from parental concerns, the conflation of assessment and funding generates an unfair professional, and indeed ethical, pressure on the individual psychologist. It is furthermore sometimes the case that, where there is an issue between the local education authority and parent/carers regarding the provision to be made, that the LEA waits until it is clear that the parents/carers are about to appeal to the special needs tribunal, and then, and only then, backs down.

Once Adam was in full-time schooling, some of the pressure upon us was relieved. It gave us breathing space during the day. However, once he returned home, everything began again, a kind of groundhog day in which the same things endlessly reoccurred on each day in a slightly different form. It should be remembered that at that time I was working as a parish priest, where enviably flexible hours are combined with the penalty of what others would experience as very unsocial hours. Specifically, the work does not finish at 5 o'clock, and I was not therefore always available to give support at a time of day when many other fathers would have been.

I will now describe life with Adam, living in family community with him. Adam was, and is, very destructive. It is no way naughtiness, but he has an urge to dismantle things, to take them apart. His brother

---

5   See for example Tenth Report of the Parliamentary Select Committee on Education and Skills in the session 2006–07. In section 20 this report asks the government for a considered response to the Committee's proposal to separate assessment from funding.

Peter, who was born in 1996, does not have many memories of this time, but remembers vividly that Adam used to break his toys if he got access to them. As will be clear, we were committed as a family to Adam's flourishing. The difficulty for us was to secure the flourishing of each and every member of the family. As well as being destructive, Adam has no sense of personal danger. He could not, because of his obsession with wires and tubes, be left unsupervised with any electrical equipment. If we left the front door open, he would go through it. Menai Bridge Vicarage was on a busy main road. We would not be able to use language to call him back. He would not understand the danger of traffic. On top of all of this Adam had a toileting problem. At the appropriate time we tried in vain to toilet train, and hoped with each year that went by that he would pass this milestone. He never has. In common with many of those with autism, Adam has a sleep problem. His sleep pattern was, and is, highly irregular. It could be argued that sleep, like toileting, is our response to the social environment in which we find ourselves. As young parents, we all expect some years of disrupted sleep. Sometimes Adam would sleep through; sometimes he would be unwilling to sleep. Once he was asleep, he might awake unexpectedly. If you combine sleeplessness with hyperactivity, destructiveness and a lack of sense of danger when awake, the extent of the problem is clear.

The battle over Adam's statement belonged to his younger years. Small children, whoever they are, only begin to give us small clues as to who they are, and who they will be. As Adam grew older, the range of challenges which he presented became more apparent, both to us his family and to professionals. The need for specialist educational provision became uncontroversial. However, as he grew older and larger, the day-to-day management of the household became more and more difficult. Tiny children, without much use of language and physically small, are picked up, carried, cared for. As time goes on, and as their language development progresses, they are controlled by an increasing array of language, including body language, on the part of their parents and carers. Adam became physically larger, but without the control over him that language would have afforded.

Thus, the issues to do with his education came gradually to take second place to the question of the level of support which he, and us his family, needed from social services. The Children Act of 1989 tells us that

> It shall be the general duty of every local authority [...] (a) to safe-guard and promote the welfare of children within their area who are in need; and (b) so far as is consistent with that duty, to pro-mote the upbringing of such children by their families, by pro-viding a range and level of services appropriate to those children's needs.[6]

As can be imagined, we looked enthusiastically within section 17 for any enforceable rights to receive services, or even to be assessed to receive services: Adam's legal rights, and our own as carers, have very much developed since this early period. Michael Mandelstam, in his book *Community Care Practice and the Law,* sets out the rather convoluted way in which, from section 17, one can actually arrive at the provision of front-line services:

> There is no explicit duty on the local authority to assess a child in need under s. 17 of the Children Act, 1989; although the Act (schedule 2) does state that an assessment under s.17 may take place at the same time as an assessment under other legislation such as s. 2 of the Chronically Sick and Disabled Persons Act 1970 (CSDPA). However, policy guidance, *Framework for the Assessment of Children in Need* assumes such a duty.[7]

Thus the duty to assess is not contained in legislation but in govern-ment guidance. *The Framework for the Assessment of Children in Need* is frank about its own legal status:

> This document is issued under section 7 of the Local Authority Social Services Act 1970, which requires local authorities in their social services functions to act under the general guidance of the Secretary of State. *As such this document does not have the full force of statute* [my italics], but should be complied with unless local cir-cumstances indicate exceptional reasons which justify a variation.

---

6   Section 17.1.
7   Mandelstam (2005), p. 277.

The courts have however shown a willingness to enforce *The Framework for the Assessment of Children in Need.*

I have taken some time here to set out in summary the basic legal framework, because I want to give an indication as to how that framework was experienced by us at the time and as events unfolded. The legislation is Byzantine in complexity and obscurity, and would be certainly beyond the grasp of many service users. Matters are further complicated by the nuanced approach of the courts, especially in regard to funding. In the middle of all of this it is true to say with Mandelstam that 'users of services have perhaps surprisingly few absolute legal rights or entitlements – although there are a few significant ones'. We found ourselves with Adam in a situation in which some of the things which we had *absolutely* taken for granted had ceased to have such a solid character. It was natural to look in those circumstances for our absolute legal rights and entitlements. We found that the legal system surrounding community care was more a mirror reflection of our predicament than our 'salvation' from it.

The two things which we most needed in order to cope with, in order to regularize, day-to-day life were regular weekly support and respite care. During school terms, the school took some of the strain, but the school holidays became an increasing struggle. These holidays coincided, of course, with Christmas and Easter, which are especially busy times in any parish. In the early years we usually got between approximately eight and twelve hours of support a week. Usually young care workers would appear, and take Adam out for a walk or for a trip in the car. For some of the care workers it was, or was very nearly, their first experience of working closely with a person with autism. After two hours or so, Adam would return, and we returned to holding the line. Often the time had been used up tackling basic household tasks which could not otherwise be undertaken. It was time away from Adam and the demands which he placed upon us, but it was not a break. The other problem was getting short breaks – time, together, away from the family home. One of the things which the social services department did was to place Adam on a short-term basis with foster carers. We were, as for the other support which we received, deeply grateful, but suspected that the families with whom Adam was placed found him just as much a challenge as we did. Sometimes, the department came across a person who was more than willing to care for Adam, but whose living accommodation was not suitable. In our own home we had by now rooms where the pictures were screwed to the wall, and where all the ornaments had been stored away in boxes. Knowing that the authorities found respite care difficult to provide, we were relieved to get away when we could, but were still tired when we returned.

Parish clergy are, in our own little way, public people, and we learn, with God's grace, to live within the public gaze, though I do not think that any priest finds it easy. I was not prepared for the way in which the 'public' would respond to a person with disabilities. A few weeks after Adam's diagnosis, we went down to visit my parents-in-law in Cwmbran in South Wales. We went out for lunch, and took Adam with us. Adam was playing with a chair in the corner of the pub, lifting it up a few inches and dropping it back onto the stone floor. As we have seen, people with autism often engage in repetitive and stereotypical behaviours, and we were only too glad that he was with us, engaged in such an activity, rather than running away. The person on the next table looked straight at Gill and said words which we had not heard before, but which are all too familiar to the parents and carers of people on the autistic spectrum: 'Can't you control your son?' Things have improved in terms of autism awareness even in this last ten years, but the words of Martin Lloyd Williams, an Anglican priest who is the father of a child with Down's syndrome, are still true: 'It is the common experience of people with disabilities and their parents or carers, that they are always being judged. We know so many parents of children on the autistic spectrum who are thoroughly disapproved of because their children are perceived to be out of control.'[8] I was thus gradually being caught in a double difficulty: being in the public gaze as a priest, but then having to respond to the not always kindly gaze with which the general public looks on those with disabilities. Autism presents particular problems in this respect, as Adam, especially when he was younger, very much looked like other children of his age: the general public, without an awareness of autism, would see his behaviours and assume that he was misbehaving. Let us take this a little further. As Adam grew, and as the hours with him rolled on into months

---

8   Williams (2007), p. 68.

and years, we were, without realizing it, getting nearer to our limit, to the end of our physical, mental, and spiritual resources, and being at that limit for all to see. It is a natural human tendency to want to believe things are better than they are. No parent gets it totally right, but there is a need to care for our children hard-wired into humanity. We were caught between having to and not being able to care. In the meantime, I was in a role of which the heart should be the giving and receiving of care.

During the Church in Wales ordination service, the Bishop asks a number of questions of those shortly to be ordained. One of the questions is this: 'Will you with your family order your life in accordance with the teachings of Christ, so that you may be a wholesome example to your people? **By the help of God, I will.**'[9] This can be the excuse for a most unattractive clerical self-righteousness. It also raises questions regarding the role of clergy families, and especially clergy wives. A generation or so ago, there was an expectation that the 'vicar's wife' would *ex officio* undertake certain duties within the parish. It was a kind of sexism which expected a woman to define herself through her husband's role. Although that no longer represents social reality it remains a reality in some people's heads. Gillian was absolutely unable to fulfil any expectations of that kind. Leaving aside these misunderstandings, Adam forced me to reflect quite hard on what it meant to order my family life, to do that in accordance with the teaching of Christ, and thus being a wholesome example to God's people. The clerical collar – as I suggested in the introduction – often prevents people from seeing the humanity of the person who wears it, from seeing that a priest can be a person with problems. I came to realize that being an example did not mean being without problems, and presenting an ordered and 'wholesome' face to the world.[10] Rather it was to be a person with problems, and showing how Christianity could present a distinctive response to those problems. This book is a working out of that insight. However, at the time I was more aware that those who saw my family life found it more troubling than inspirational. We all want to believe that the world is a more wonderful, more blessed place than it often is and try to block out anything which

---

9   *The Book of Common Prayer* (1984), p. 724.

10   See above, p. 17.

provides evidence to the contrary. As T.S. Eliot wrote in the Four Quartets: 'Human kind cannot bear too much reality.' A good friend had given me a present at the time of my ordination, a book by Sarah Horsman, *Living With Stress – a guide for ministers and church leaders*. I still have this, but probably did not at the time recognize ourselves described in its pages:

> Major illness or disability within the family can be a source of stress which is hidden from public view. Short-term illnesses are often met with a good deal of sympathy and practical help. But it soon runs out in the face of long term disability; the family may be thrown back on their own resources, and faced with a major drain on time, money and energy. Regular, practical help and emotional support will be much needed, and extra care when moving ministers who are caught up in this situation. Mental illness, personality or behavioural problems tend to make people feel uncomfortable. When a minister or his children or spouse suffer from such problems, people will have even more difficulty in knowing how to respond. The family which needs extra support may well be the one which gets most isolated.[11]

Elsewhere in this book, I will trace the comprehensive challenges that life with Adam presented to almost any theological and philosophical statement. Aware of this, and worn down, preaching became more and more difficult. Although I have had other troubles down the years – as everyone does – this was the first time that I had known the depths. I was worried that, knowing those depths, I was becoming an apologist for God: trying to justify the ways of God to humanity came to seem very much like justifying the unjustifiable: if God is active in the world why is it like this; if God is not active, why not? As a priest, one is aware that things which we say – a single word, a single sentence – may have the capacity to change the course of the life of the hearer. As priests, we depend on those words having an authentic correspondence with what is in our hearts. Furthermore pastoral care involves being alongside people in the most difficult of circumstances, as well as at times of extreme joy. It is, in ways which are not generally recognized, enormously consuming of energy. I was afraid of giving away what little energy I had left.

---

11   Horsman (1989), p. 63.

In these circumstances, I decided upon a radical change of direction. A post was advertised as National Co-ordinator in Wales for the National Autistic Society. I applied and got the job. It involved a move down to South Wales to be near enough the office in Neath. This suited, because I had also become aware of the provision offered by Heronsbridge School in Bridgend. In July of 2002, Estyn – the Welsh equivalent of Ofsted – published a report on the school, of which these were some of the main findings.

> Heronsbridge is a very good school. It has built on the good start reported by the previous inspection in 1997. It now has many outstanding features and it is very successful in meeting its pupils' wide range of SEN [special educational needs] and enabling them to achieve as much as they can. Progress made by the school in recent years is due to exceptional leadership and the dedicated hard work of all the staff. The school is rare in that it combines rigour in assessing and analysing the performance of its pupils with an ethos that is extremely caring, open and friendly. Pupils who attend Heronsbridge receive special education of the highest quality.

The work with Adam in Ysgol y Bont had been exceptional: at about this time we nominated Adam's teacher for the Guardian special needs teacher of the year award, and were delighted when she won the Welsh round. However, the attractions of Heronsbridge, and especially its five day a week residential provision, were obvious. The trouble was that until a move had actually taken place it was difficult to negotiate exactly what support he would need.

The move to Bridgend at the end of 2002 was traumatic. Rather than starting with our family response to this, I will start with Adam. People with autism like order, regularity, and familiarity. It has to be said that we were warned by many that a move would be traumatic for him. What actually happened was that many of his behaviours were accentuated, and his use of language – exiguous at best – retreated. We struggled to find an appropriate house in Bridgend, because we needed a home where the physical geography of the building would allow us to give at least one downstairs room to Adam, as well as his sleeping accommodation upstairs. We eventually found a place at a price affordable to us, but with the problem that we would have to wait until a part-exchange had been completed, and the developer had built a new house for the family who were moving out. As a result we had to move into rented accommodation. It had been difficult enough when Adam was living in a vicarage. In our rented house, we watched him tear down blinds, tear wallpaper, and urinate on the carpet. Legally, nobody could refuse to rent the house to us on the grounds of Adam's disability, but we could be and were expected to pay for the damage which resulted.

By Christmas, we had all arrived. We lasted another couple of months. One night in February, we had the most traumatic night. Adam was on his feet for what seemed all night long. In the small hours, I agreed with Gillian that we would take one hour on and one hour off. I promised her that in the course of the following day, matters would be resolved. At about seven o'clock (the times are *very* approximate) I rang the out of hours service for social services. As ever they advised me that they could do very little at that time of the morning, and advised me to contact the office during working hours. A very old friend from college, Fr. Edwin Counsell was the Anglican parish priest in a nearby parish in the Vale of Glamorgan. In the months since our arrival he had become even more familiar with our situation. I telephoned him, saying that it was impossible to carry on like this, and asking, as I was so very tired, if he would come with me to approach social services. I waited until Adam was on his way to school, and knew that I now had until four o'clock. Edwin and I met in the lobby of the local social services department, in a block appropriately known as 'Sunnyside', at about 8.30. Once people had clocked in, we approached the reception desk and explained the circumstances. I said weakly that the matter would need to be sorted out in the course of that day. Just after nine o'clock a messenger came down to say that everybody was in meetings until midday. In my tiredness, I do not think in retrospect that I had made what I was trying to say clear: that people would need to start work at nine o'clock in order to have any chance of resolving things in the course of the day. I always try to be courteous, but this was too much. A last ember flared, as I looked straight back, and uttered the words 'now is now'. The messenger, no doubt wearily accustomed to the hostile behaviours of social services clients, looked back, and was about to answer. Then she retreated.

The day was as long as the night. Having by that stage had a number of bruising encounters with social services both on Anglesey and in Bridgend, I knew that the outcome was not a foregone conclusion. I did not know what we were going to do if at the end of school day Adam was to be returned to our care. However, by the end of the day Adam found himself temporarily accommodated in a respite unit a couple of miles from our home. A few weeks later, as another resident was being moved to adult services, a vacancy arose at the residential unit in Heronsbridge school. Until we left Bridgend, Adam spent his weekdays at Heronsbridge, and his weekends at the respite unit, though there was some concern expressed that the unit was being used in a way not in keeping with its statement of purpose. As parents who had needed respite care down the years, we were also concerned about parents who would not be able to access the facility because Adam was, full-time, taking up a bedroom. Then, in about the April, we got the key to our new home in Bridgend. For the first time in my life, I was a proud house owner, but a member of my family was elsewhere.

Adam was accommodated by the local authority under section 20 of the Children Act. That section obliges the authority to provide accommodation where '(c) the person who has been caring for him being prevented (whether or not permanently, and for whatever reason) from providing him with suitable accommodation or care'. The arrangement was on a voluntary basis – technically we could have had Adam home at a time of our choosing. The great principle of the Children's Act is that the interests of the child should, however, be paramount. In the first place, Adam also entered the LAC – Looked After Children – system. I looked upon this, insofar as I had the energy to think about it at all, with some suspicion. In everything, there was a profound loss of control, and the idea that there was a regular review meeting at which many others, apart from ourselves as his parents, would be taking decisions about Adam's future, contributed very much to this sense. However, the LAC system has, and had here, some important benefits. The review meeting, alongside the other professionals, has an independent chair, whose responsibility it is to look with some objectivity at any given situation, and, if necessary, to 'speak truth to power'. I am not saying that at this point we sat back, but the system as it began to work took a pressure off us which had otherwise been crushing.

It would however be good to think that this was the beginning of a new and better time. It is in the nature of post-traumatic stress that it bites after the event. In the midst of extreme, and potentially overwhelming stress, many of us keep going. As Winston Churchill is believed to have said: 'When you are going through hell, keep going.' The hell had been created by the need to care for our son: naturally we would, in those circumstances, keep going, keep caring, even when that became almost unbearable. Once Adam was in full-time care, things were different. I had a job which involved autism: between home life and work, wherever I looked, there was autism. My capacity to handle either work or family life properly was compromised by mental, physical and – I would say – spiritual exhaustion. By November, I was off work, and being medicated for stress and depression. In January, following a highly constructive meeting with my manager, I was no longer working. The National Autistic Society arranged some meetings with a secular counsellor. I still gratefully regard these counselling sessions as some kind of turning point.

Down the years, I have met clergy who exude a brash, spiritual self confidence. I have also met clergy who are deeply wounded and broken, including, it has to be said, clergy who have undergone that experience because of the ferocity of the current debates within the Anglican communion about human sexuality. I am deeply suspicious of the former, and turn naturally to the latter, because I see in that woundedness and brokenness something which belongs to the heart of the Gospel. I am aware that it is not easy for anybody, let alone a priest, to admit to mental health problems, even if they are – as in my case, as I would like to think – triggered by circumstances which would have driven almost anybody in the same direction. A report published in July 2008 by the All-party Parliamentary Group on Mental Health revealed the results of a survey that one out of five members of Parliament had undergone difficulties with their mental health, while one third of those MPs, peers and Parliamentary staff who responded to the survey 'saw work based stigma and a hostile reaction from the media and general population as barriers to openess about mental health issues'.[12] Our society treats those with mental health problems as different, as threatening. We do not realize, for example, that depression can be interpreted as being a 'normal', 'natural' response to the fact of simply being alive. Adam had sent me to that place, but it was in that place that I came to appreciate in a far richer way what it is like to be Adam, to be the excluded other which our society both pities and dreads. There is not much in literature which describes adequately my state of mind at this time. The best description of all comes from another priest, also formed in the Catholic tradition, Gerald Manley Hopkins, in words for which I will not offer interpretation, but rather simply allow them to speak for themselves:

> No worst, there is none. Pitched past pitch of grief,
> More pangs will, schooled at forepangs, wilder wring.
> Comforter, where, where is your comforting?
> Mary, mother of us, where is your relief?
> My cries heave, herds-long; huddle in a main, a chief
> Woe, world-sorrow; on an age-old anvil wince and sing –
> Then lull, then leave off. Fury had shrieked 'No ling-ering!
> Let me be fell: force I must be brief'.
>
> O the mind, mind has mountains; cliffs of fall
> Frightful, sheer, no-man-fathomed. Hold them cheap
> May who ne'er hung there. Nor does long our small
> Durance deal with that steep or deep. Here! creep,
> Wretch, under a comfort serves in a whirlwind: all
> Life death does end and each day dies with sleep.[13]

Even the most cursory reader of this book will become aware that I am an enthusiast for living and thinking. For once, by the January of 2004 my way of being in the world was different. I could not see a way back or a way forward. Throughout my time in Bridgend, I had carried on preaching on Sundays, and enjoyed the welcome which I had received from local congregations, in Cardiff, in the Vale of Glamorgan, and in the Valleys. I had left full-time ministry with a sense of frustration about the Church's unwillingness to engage in

---

12   All-party Parliamentary Group on Mental Health (2008), p. 2. The survey did not include the members of the House of Lords who were judges or bishops.

13   Hopkins (ed.) (1953), p. 61.

the issues which really matter in people's everyday lives. Yet I had by now discovered that the capacity of the political system to deliver the real, lasting and urgent changes which are needed was limited, that the political system is itself disabled. That all sounds rather negative – as if the whole process hinged around what the Church or wider society will not, or cannot, accomplish. More positively many priests and indeed many Christians would speak of a sense of calling that will not let go, leaving only the question of the extent and quality of our own response. Reflecting on all these things, I did not want to rush back into full-time ministry even if the opportunity arose: apart from anything else I needed time to recharge my batteries.

In about May of 2004, I went to see Carl Cooper, at that time the Bishop of St. David's Diocese, whom I had known since my time in North Wales in the Diocese of Bangor. He listened with enormous, and frankly moving, care and concern to some of the story. He told me that he had a vacancy in the Parish of Llangeler with Penboyr. By July I found myself – *I found myself* – as the priest in charge of five churches in the Teifi valley in West Wales, in the heart of the Welsh countryside. It is a myth that the countryside is a quiet place. People live here and work hard here. However, this area has an undeniable beauty, and places within it which are places of great quiet. This was where I needed to be, not as a luxury, but indeed as a necessity. The move left the anomalous situation that Adam was living and being cared for in Bridgend, while this came to be – as far as I am aware – paid for by Carmarthenshire County Council. In Wales there are 22 relatively small such local authorities in a small country, so even the slightest move can generate a situation of that kind. We could detect a certain tension between the authorities, a keenness that Adam should move on. We were very impressed by the carefulness with which Carmarthenshire planned for Adam's future and explored different options for him. They took his needs as paramount, and were, like us, concerned that any placement should be successful. After the trauma of his previous move to Bridgend, the last thing which Adam needed was a move followed by placement breakdown, and a subsequent enforced move. After other options had been excluded, it was decided to place him at Rowden House, a full-time residential school in Herefordshire. After we moved from Bridgend, but before he moved to Herefordshire, he had also received an additional diagnosis of attention deficit hyper-activity disorder. According to the reports of his carers, on some of the measures of hyperactivity on the Connor scale (which measures such things) he had a higher score than the scale allows for.

When, as I am now, sitting in the vicarage in Llangeler, I go, in my mind's eye, to his room in Herefordshire. Around that room, this book revolves. Everything has been done to make the space appropriate for him. On the right-hand side as you go in, there is a range of built-in wardrobes. These have to be opened with a daisy key, because other-wise Adam would go and pull things out from them. At the end of this range, there is a cupboard, with a glass screen window through which he can safely see his television. The floor is not carpeted. Within weeks of his arrival the existing carpet became soaked in urine, and had to be thrown out. The bed is built into the wall and floor, with a waterproof mattress. On the far wall of the room is a large canvas which Adam had – with assistance – painted when he was in Bridgend. It is highly abstract and colourful. On the opposite wall, behind a perspex frame which is tightly screwed to the wall, there are photographs of many of his immediate family members, including his grandparents. Gill's parents sadly died after he moved to the school. Adam was told about this, but we have never wanted to remove their photographs from his wall. A person with autism appreciates that regularity and continuity.

We try to go on a regular basis to Adam's school. On average we probably see him about once a month. His younger brother Peter is always keen to see him, but only really has an opportunity to do so during the school holidays, and on the two occasions in the year when Adam comes over to see us. The safety of car transport for Adam has recently been reassessed, and he now has three people with him whenever he is driven in the car: one to drive and two to manage his behaviour, to stop him, for example, winding the windows down, or opening the car doors when the car is moving, if child-safety locks are not available. Although the home visits are important, it is much easier for us to go to him than for him to come to us.

The school has very much operated an open-door policy, and has been mindful of how psychologically difficult it is to have a close family member of Adam's age living in another place, and in the day-to-day care of others. Within reasonable limits, and having regard to the safety and privacy of other residents, we are encouraged to be with him in his home there, as we would be if he was in our home. The staff have always been without exception open and welcoming and open to question. One of the psychological responses to the loss of parental control is to assert control over the situation. We have tried to avoid doing that, and to acknowledge the wisdom and care of the staff in the day-to-day decisions which are made for Adam's welfare. On a weekly basis we receive a letter from the school, as it were in Adam's voice, giving us a report upon his activities.

Adam is changing and developing. The most recent development is that he has arrived at adolescence. This is traumatic to a greater or lesser extent for all, and Adam is not exempt from this. It is a time when communication often breaks down – albeit temporarily – between parent and child. In Adam's case he is changing both emotionally and biologically, but without the opportunity to discuss that on a reciprocal basis with others. It is probable that he does not understand what is happening to him. It is the first time in his life where I have felt that he is 'suffering' from autism. Over this period, he became increasingly stressed, and his sleep problems, which always have been considerable – either not sleeping, or awaking at unpredictable times at night, with corresponding tiredness the following day – became acute. These things were always a source of great strain to us as a family; even with highly conscientious staff, working in shifts, they can produce pressure on a caring institution. We have most recently been discussing with the school and with others involved in Adam's care the question of whether or not to use medication, and changes in medication, to calm his challenging behaviours,[14] and to improve his sleep patterns. Parenthood by committee, once you get used to it, is a wonderful thing: it works well with the high levels of mutual trust that have been built up in this situation. Everyone is working in a mutually supportive way on a range of problems which we all recognize to be difficult.

We now know, as Adam's parents, that we will never be free of issues connected with his care, and the issues are usually not small

---

14   In Adam's case, this takes the form of hyperactivity and self-injurious behaviour. One should be alert to the fact that when this term is used it can cover a range of very diverse behaviours, and hence lack a necessary clarity.

ones. We are both now middle aged. Like so many others in our situation we are concerned about what will happen to Adam when we are no longer able to visit him or to take an active role in his care. We are so pleased to see the love and care which Peter shows on our visits to Adam, because it may well be that it is Peter that will exercise our responsibilities in later years. Yet he cannot be made to take that responsibility, and if pressure were to be put upon him to do so, he would – quite rightly – react against it. That being said, we try to make sure that he is as well informed as possible for one of his age on the issues to do with Adam's care. Once Adam passed his fourteenth birthday, it became a legal responsibility on all concerned in his annual educational review to begin planning for his transition into adult services. In the earlier years, because of the educational component, funding can be relatively generous. Adult services are generally financed by social services. Social care is perennially underfunded. If any reader who cares for an elderly relative has experienced the limitation of services in domiciliary care, they will be aware of the circumstances which may constrain the provision for Adam in his later years. In those years, the same principles will apply to Adam's care as will have applied throughout his life. In St. John's Gospel, Jesus speaks of coming to the world 'that you might have life, and have it more abundantly'.[15] Living is good, but, in itself, not enough. One would not have to be a member of the Christian community to believe that the life which we are all meant to live is what may be called 'the abundant life'. The question remains of how one would describe, for Adam, 'abundant life'. For his own safety he needs constant control and supervision, especially as he grows physically larger: it would be sad if in his adult years the need for control and supervision was to be so overwhelming that it pushed out the rest of that abundant life.

In concluding this chapter, I shall look back over these experiences, which unfolded during the last ten years, and ask of myself the question: 'How do I feel?' The irony is that such a question could be supremely difficult for a person with autism, but it is actually a difficult question for so many of us to answer honestly, in the privacy of our own hearts and before others. If I say that I feel angry, I will need to say more. All of us have a persona which we present to the world,

---

15   John 10:10.

the way in which we register in the worlds of others. There are those who are seen as angry people. I do not believe that people who meet me from day to day think that of me. In my pastoral work, I use a lot of humour, because I know, if deployed sensibly, it simply cheers people up. If anything, in day-to-day contact, I would like to think that because I have known extreme pain myself, I am cautious about creating it for others. I try to be so. Yet, I am angry in ways which go deeper than aggressive behaviour. Many parents and carers faced with extreme situations take their anger out on the many professionals whom they meet, of whom some, and I would like to think the vast majority, are doing their best to help. The anger I have today is no longer, if it ever was, directed at individuals. I am angry with a world in which such things could be; I am thus angry with God, in the way that Job was; I am angry with the Church (and, honestly, with my own denomination) for substituting all manner of concerns for the priority which Jesus gives to the Samaritan's practical care for those in the greatest need; I am angry with the political world for abandoning the high ideals of a welfare State to the vagaries of a market economy. Of all this, I will say more later. For now, let me say this. It is possible to listen to debates in General Synod, or in Westminster, and in many other places, where profound, real anger is expressed. These days, I listen to that kind of anger, and know that I am more angry, and that I am way beyond suppressing that anger. I hope it is not dishonest of me to say that if you met me from day to day, you would never guess.

The reason that you would never guess may be this. I am not whatever we may mean by the term 'fundamentalist'. Temperamentally, I do not generally appeal to absolutes. Adam's life has however taught me the *absolute* priority of care and kindness, indeed of love, over all things, and over all other values. In regard to those things, I am a fundamentalist. Philosophically, it is an *a priori*. As we will see in the next chapter, holding on to this as an absolute does not spare me from uncertainty and doubt.

Looking over this chapter, which is intended to be a biography of Adam, I can see that much of it is about our response to him as parents, about our own feelings and concerns, rather than about Adam himself. I suspect that this is the effect of living in a family one of whose members is almost wordless, but I hope that this chapter will indeed stand as his biography.

CHAPTER 3

■———————————————————————————■

The Why Question

In the last chapter I described an extreme situation, which continued and developed over a period of years. This chapter represents the beginnings of a spiritual response. It tries to describe a prayerful self awareness in the presence, of God, in whose presence the question 'why?' is asked. This attempt at prayerful self awareness is the basis of all that follows, the reflection upon Scripture, liturgy, systematic theology, ecclesiology, politics, law and economics. Because of Adam, I had to begin at the beginning, to hold on to faith as though I had never held on to it before, and, above all, to question everything.

The experience thus became, in Paul Tillich's words, an experience of 'meaning within meaninglessness, of certitude within doubt'. Tillich found this, not in 'the God of traditional Theism, but the "God above God", the power of being, which works through those who have no name for it, not even the name god'.[1] It will be understood, in our very particular family circumstances, that this unnamed God, whose name is not verbalized, has, as deities go, a certain appeal. 'This is the answer', continues Tillich, 'to those who ask for a message in the nothingness of their situation and at the end of their courage to be. But such an extreme point is not a space within which one can live. *The dialectics of an extreme situation are a criterion of truth but not the basis on which a whole structure of truth can be built*' [my italics].[2] I would want to distinguish here between two things: the extreme situation

---

1   Tillich (ed.) (1978), p. 14.
2   Ibid.

in which we found ourselves as a family as a result of Adam's autism, and Adam's autism itself. From the former we have moved on; from the latter, as autism is a lifelong condition, Adam will never move on. I would want to insist with Tillich that the extreme situation is 'a criterion of truth'. I would agree with Tillich that it is not the sole criterion of truth. However, for Adam, that extremity, that marginality has to be the basis on which a whole structure of truth can be built. Theologians, philosophers and politicians predicate their work on assumptions about human nature, about what humanity is. Whenever we formulate a sentence with the structure 'humanity is...' we need to fulfil the ostensible intention of such a sentence. We must not inadvertently omit some of humanity. Adam, and many others whose life is characterized by difference, have to be included, in whatever way we finish the sentence.

There are three occasions during Adam's life when I hit the depths. The first was on the day of his diagnosis, at the very end of the day. The second occasion was at the end of the day on which we asked Adam to be taken into full-time care. The third occasion was when my own mental health collapsed into stress and depression at the end of that same year. I was, on that third occasion, as Tillich says, 'at the end of my courage to be'. These are acutely painful memories which will remain with me for the rest of my life. The natural question which is asked by so many in such extreme situations is 'why is the world like this?'. The classic formulation of that question is given in John Hick's *Evil and the God of Love*:

> The problem dealt with in this book is [...] a theological one: can the presence of evil in the world be reconciled with the existence of a God who is unlimited both in goodness and in power? This is a problem equally for the believer and for the non-believer. In the mind of the latter it stands as a major obstacle to religious commitment, whilst for the former it sets up an acute internal tension to disturb his [sic] faith and to lay upon it a perpetual burden of doubt.[3]

This programmatic statement for Hick's work merits some unpacking. In dealing with the effects upon myself and upon my family of these

---

3   Hick (1985), p. 3.

extreme circumstances it would be natural enough to turn to that considerable literature on the so called 'problem of evil' of which Hick's book forms a part. However, and however difficult our circumstances were – and will be – I was highly reluctant to describe them as part of the 'evil' which exists in the world. It would be tantamount to failing to accept my son for who he is and as he is. Such a description would be part of a wider rhetoric of disability which treats those who are disabled as victims of a tragedy. This in turn is part of the tendency of wider society to hold disabled people, and perhaps especially the severely disabled, at arm's length. Adam and his like are often a disturbing presence within the world.

We need also to look carefully at those words 'goodness' and 'power', especially in their application to God. God is given by humanity a range of attributes: as nobody has ever seen God,[4] when we think of His 'goodness' and 'power', we necessarily use human analogies. We think of goodness as shown through, among other things, the lives of people we have known; we think of power by using examples of the way in which power is exercised by humans over each other. Nietzsche spoke famously of going beyond good and evil. We do not need Nietzsche in order to make this move. Subsequent Christian reflection has obscured the extent to which Jesus himself was the solvent of traditional moral distinctions. The communities in which he lived had a strong sense of moral purity/impurity, of cleanliness/uncleanliness. Jesus himself ran counter to such strong binary distinctions, in his willingness to associate with the excluded, with sinners and with lepers. His proclamation of forgiveness has historically been interpreted as reinforcing strong moral code, a regime of goodness. One may suspect that in its original social context it was the solvent of such a regime, allowing those whose life had not been characterized by goodness to have access to its privileges. Similarly with power. Christ's own teaching is a solvent of power as such, a critique not just of the way in which sovereignty is exercised, but of sovereignty itself:

> A dispute also arose among them, which of them was to be regarded as the greatest. And he said to them, 'The kings of the

---

4   1 John 4:12.

Gentiles exercise lordship over them; and those in authority over them are called benefactors. But not so with you; rather let the greatest among you become as the youngest, and the leader as one who serves. For which is the greater, one who sits at table, or one who serves? Is it not the one who sits at table? But I am among you as one who serves.'[5]

Jesus calls both goodness and power to transformation. When we lay the attributes of goodness and power upon God, and use the model of humanity for that, we need to have regard not simply to humanity as it is, but as it is called to be. God's power comprehends weakness, God's goodness comprehends that which is not good. When Hick talks of 'unlimited' goodness and power, he is not thinking of this, but rather of power, without remainder, goodness without remainder. Once we think differently about goodness and power the problem which he poses is not so great.

However, we also need to take the question further back, and look at the creation itself. The universe and autism, which is a part of the universe, have this in common: we do not know what causes them.[6] Within that uncertainty, I would affirm the traditional Christian view of the creation of the world from nothing 'ex nihilo' which is – despite the fires of controversy – not altogether dissimilar to what is known as 'big bang theory'. I cannot see the Genesis account as being anything other than a highly attractive story which allows us to reflect upon the mystery of creation. It was never intended to be a scientific theory in the modern sense, and it is unfair to the text to set it up as if it was. The theological account of creation makes valuations and evaluations, rather than concerning itself with scientifically accurate physics, chemistry and biology. We have just seen that the way in which the traditional Christian witness which attributes perfection, and indeed perfections, to God is problematic, but alongside that goes an inheritance from the Judaeo-Christian tradition which refuses to attribute the same perfection to God's creation. In the account in the first chapter of Genesis, God sees what he is said to have made, and behold, it is very good.[7] Excellence – 'very good' – does not mean perfection.

---

5   Luke 22:24–27.
6   See Chapter 1, 'What is autism?', p. 23f.
7   Verse 31.

We can assemble a series of questions like this:

1. If creation had been perfect, rather than very good, would it have included autism, and thence people with autism? I believe the answer to that to be yes, not on rational grounds – it is difficult enough rationally to grasp this world, let alone a never-existent alternative – but simply as intuition.

2. Did the prelapsarian excellence of God's creation include autism? I believe that it did, for reasons which I will examine.

3. Is the existence of autism and other disabilities to be attributed to the fallen nature of humanity as described in the Book of Genesis? I believe not, because I have a general concern about associating disability with ill-health in a medical model of disability, and about the further step of associating ill-health with sinfulness. There is an argument that all human beings are made in the image and likeness of God, but that image and likeness is marred by human sinfulness. I could not believe that Adam's autism in any way mars the image and likeness of God in him.

In this last point, I am deliberately contradicting the preparatory statement of the Committee for the Jubilee Day of the Community with Persons with Disabilities, which took place on 3 December 2000. Part one of this statement deals with 'The person with disabilities: the image of God and a place of his wonders'. The wonder does not extend to excluding disability from inclusion in the consequences of the Fall:

> Fragility, sickness, pain, disability, solitude and death are seen as acts of injustice by God, but it is precisely sin – the abuse of freedom – which causes these dramatic limitations. We must say however, that the sin of our first parents with all its consequences and responsibilities had the power to dim, although not eliminate, this image, which God blessed from the beginning.[8]

---

8   http://www.vatican.va/jubilee_2000/jubilevents/jub_disabled_20001203_ scheda1_en.htm [accessed 21 February 2009].

I talk elsewhere about a sense of meaninglessness and nothingness belonging not to Adam, but to the experience of caring for him. I would suggest that when God made things out of nothing, some of that nothingness inhered in the creation. There is, therefore, nothing wrong with nothingness – it is very good, it is the stuff of creation.

Let us look in more specific detail at the link between the story of creation and autism. It will be recalled that in autism there are a triad of impairments, to do with socialization, language and lastly with imagination and play. If we ask the question as to why God created the universe, we are, within a traditional Christian framework, brought up against that triad of impairments. The effect of creation is that God is no longer alone: he overcomes his cosmic solitude. With the coming to being of humanity, God is committed to socialization. This is expressed in the reciprocity of the covenant theology of the Old Testament, and thence in the new covenant which is in Christ Jesus. Alongside this comes the question of language. St. John's Gospel in its prologue teaches the co-eternity of the Word, of Christ, deliberately echoing the first words of the book of Genesis: 'In the beginning was the Word, and the Word was with God, and the Word was God. The same was in the beginning with God. All things were made by him; and without him was not any thing made that was made.'[9] Language as such is prior to creation and lies at the heart of creation. If at the moment of creation language is there, and socialization comes to be, creation itself can be interpreted, following Moltmann, as play. In a passage entitled 'Play as symbol of the world' Moltmann speaks of the Wisdom tradition of the Old Testament:

> According to this tradition, the creation of the world has the character of play, which gives God delight and human beings joy. This means that the world does not exist out of necessity. It exists because God created it out of liberty. He created it freely, but not arbitrarily. So the world is not a matter of chance. He created what gives him pleasure, and what gives him pleasure is what accords with his inmost nature. That is why God's creation is a good creation. This unity of free creation and the pleasure that belongs to God's own nature is best described through the category of play.

---

9   John 1:1–3.

Moltmann then continues by seeing play not only in creation but in redemption: 'The Redeemer plays a wonderful game of love with the beloved soul, in order to redeem her in liberty.'[10] If this line of thinking is correct, then the creation is not simply the free play of God, it is also His powerfully imaginative play: he imagined it, and behold, it was. There are two ways to proceed from here. We live in a culture and society that treats autism as a problematic. In one way only this is fortunate: the problematization of autism leads, by an often long road, but not without fail, to a society which seeks to meet more effectively the needs of people with autism and their carers. However, we may suspect that people are not aware of the cosmic profundity of the problem which autism presents. There is however another way of approaching matters, for those with autism and their carers who may well have had quite enough of being treated as a problem, cosmic or otherwise. It is to suggest that because language, socialization and play belong so closely to the order of creation, then their other – the triad of 'impairments' – belong there too. It is because creation is what creation is that the triad of impairments are what they are. It may be that creation is what it is because of the triad of impairments. Be that as it may, within traditional Christian thought, had God been a God with autism, creation would not have been.

Having had the most profound difficulty in locating Adam within a particular set of ideas, I will now attempt to say where I do locate him. It is at this point that my own capacity of using expressive language begins to collapse. I was once asked whether I considered Adam, as well as the other members of my family, as a blessing from God. The question, unbeknown presumably to the questioner, and certainly to myself at the time, is the reflection of an old folk belief. As Barr pointed out as long ago as 1904 in his *Mental Defectives – their history, treatment and training,* there are some societies in which a house into which an 'imbecile'[11] was born was considered blessed by God.[12] I cannot remember my reply when the question was put, beyond knowing that it was a well intentioned question, and yet thinking it to be

---

10   Moltmann (1985), pp. 310–312, p. 311.

11   This is, of course, Barr's terminology rather than my own.

12   Cited by Margaret A. Winzer, in her contribution to *The Disability Studies Reader:* 'Disability and society before the eighteenth century – dread and despair.' Davis (ed.) (1997), p. 92.

an extraordinarily difficult question. It is indeed more than that. In the answer to it, language betrays its own weakness: neither 'yes', nor 'no', nor 'perhaps' is the appropriate answer. I do know that the three moments of 'hitting the depths' which I have just described – alongside others – remain as experiences of total negativity, of nothingness, of meaninglessness. I had heard the phrase 'the dark night of the soul' in theological discourse. To live all the way through that night is different. I am in a different place now. However, I do not allow being in a different place to change or challenge the integrity of those moments. Meaningless they were, and meaningless they remain. To believe anything other would be to belittle those moments, to belittle their significance. Yet their significance is still their meaninglessness, without remainder.

In his witty and therefore entertaining book *The God Delusion* (2006), which sadly is marred by sharing the stridency and rhetoric virulence of the religious figures that it seeks to attack, Richard Dawkins offers a spectrum of religious belief/unbelief. From Dawkins' point of view, theism – like autism – would seem to be a spectrum disorder:

1. Strong theist. 100% probability of God. In the words of C.G. Jung: 'I do not believe, I know.'

2. Very high probability but short of 100%. *De facto* theist. 'I cannot know for certain, but I strongly believe in God, and live my life on the assumption that he is there.'

3. Higher than 50% but not very high. Technically agnostic but leaning towards theism. 'I am very uncertain, but I am inclined to believe in God.'

4. Exactly 50%. Completely impartial agnostic. 'God's existence and non-existence are equally equiprobable.'

5. Lower than 50% but not very low. Technically agnostic but leaning towards atheism. 'I don't know whether God exists, but I am inclined to be sceptical.'

6. Very low probability but short of zero. *De facto* atheist. 'I cannot

know for certain, but I think that God is very improbable, and I live my life on the assumption that he is not there.'

7. Strong atheist. I know there is no God, with the same conviction as Jung 'knows' there is one.

Dawkins acknowledges that what he is describing here is a continuous spectrum, but there must surely be a difficulty in trying to describe such a nuanced thing as religious belief within the terms of such a strict categorization. Moreover, there are unspoken theological difficulties in his very language. To say that God either is or is not 'there' is to fall into the error – which would be an error regardless of whether one was a theist or an atheist – of making God into one of the objects within the cosmos. Like a chair or a tree he is either 'there' or he is not. God's very being is much, much more than our sense of his 'thereness'. Moreover, Dawkins does not do justice in the way that he describes faith to the fundamental Christian insight that God, rather than being there, is here, immediately present to us. It is exactly His 'hereness' and 'thereness' which allows him to transcend the simple status of another object with His world. With all these reservations, I now seek to apply the Dawkins' scale of faithfulness. On this scale, I would place myself, if pressed and only if pressed, and as I am now at (2): 'Very high probability but short of 100%. *De facto* theist. "I cannot know for certain, but I strongly believe in God, and live my life on the assumption that he is there."' One might say that this is the view of a professional cleric: 'he would say that, wouldn't he' – I am nonetheless aware that it remained my basic view throughout the period when I was not working for the Church. However, I do not believe that this tells the whole story, it simplifies the reality of faith, and we are often pushed into such simplifications. The key comes in Dawkins' use of the word 'spectrum'. He uses this metaphor purposely to indicate that this is a sliding scale, in which one level of faith shades off into another. However, perhaps inadvertently, there is a kind of dogmatism behind it. Although the colours of the spectrum merge into each other, they also mutually exclude each other: red cannot be yellow, and so forth. I would want to argue that it is possible to locate oneself simultaneously at different points on the spectrum. I seek to live my life on the assumption that there is a God, but I want fiercely to maintain the integrity of those moments when God was not, in Dawkins' terms, 'there'. In this we — Christians and non-believers — have a model in the words of Christ himself on the cross: 'My God, my God, why have you forsaken me?'[13] This is clearly the statement of a strong theist, but one for whom at that moment God was not 'there'. The acuity of mental and/or physical pain is an experience common to theist and atheist alike.

Those who go through extreme experiences of any kind are driven in either of two directions. There are those who are driven to a sense of utter dependence upon God. On so many occasions, I have heard those in my pastoral care utter words like these: 'I don't know how I coped. We get our strength from somewhere. God helped and sustained me.' This is a popular spirituality which is reflected in the prayers of the Church. We can just take one example amongst so much else from the Gelasian Sacramentary: 'Almighty and everlasting God, the comfort of the sad, the strength of those who suffer; hear the prayers of your children who cry out of any trouble, and to every distressed soul grant mercy, relief, and refreshment, through Jesus Christ our Lord. Amen.' On the other hand, there are those who escape from the classic co-nundrum posed by John Hick, by saying that they cannot believe that a powerful and all-loving good God would allow such suffering to happen. Anthony Flew, in his famous and much discussed short article back in 1950 *Theology and Falsification*, gave a memorable phrase: 'His earthly father is driven frantic in his efforts to help, but his Heavenly Father reveals no obvious sign of concern.'[14] I did not find myself — and in some senses I was the observer of the process here rather than being an active participant in it — going in either of these two direc-tions, to or away from faith, but rather to a place which was and is beyond the well-rehearsed binary divisions between the sacred and the secular, faith and unfaith. I believe that this process lies at the heart of a classically orthodox Christian faith. In the year 451, the Fathers of the Church assembled for the Council of Chalcedon. Against the monophysites, who held that Christ had only one nature (physis), the Council held that the Christ had two natures, both human and divine.

---

13   Mark 15:34 with Matthew 27:46.
14   Reprinted many times, but here from Hick (ed.) (1964), pp. 224–228, this at p. 227.

The text of the Council shows the Fathers wrestling at the limits of language to put something of eternal importance into words:

> Following the holy Fathers we teach with one voice that the Son [of God] and our Lord Jesus Christ is to be confessed as one and the same [Person], that he is perfect in Godhead and perfect in manhood, very God and very man, of a reasonable soul and [human] body consisting, consubstantial with the Father as touching his Godhead, and consubstantial with us as touching his manhood; made in all things like unto us, sin only excepted; begotten of his Father before the worlds according to his Godhead; but in these last days for us men and for our salvation born [into the world] of the Virgin Mary, the Mother of God according to his manhood. This one and the same Jesus Christ, the only-begotten Son [of God] must be confessed to be in two natures, unconfusedly, immutably, indivisibly, inseparably [united], and that without the distinction of natures being taken away by such union, but rather the peculiar property of each nature being preserved and being united in one Person and subsistence, not separated or divided into two persons, but one and the same Son and only-begotten, God the Word, our Lord Jesus Christ, as the Prophets of old time have spoken concerning him, and as the Lord Jesus Christ hath taught us, and as the Creed of the Fathers hath delivered to us.

The consequence of this doctrine is that when we gaze on a crucifix, or imagine the scene of the cross in our mind's eye, we see two things simultaneously: we see a human being dying; we see God dying. On the ground of embodied suffering there is a meeting between the human and the divine, the sacred and the secular, the meaningful and the meaningless. To return to Christ's cry from the cross – 'My God, my God, why have you forsaken me?' – we hear meaningfulness and meaninglessness fused together in one moment. In orthodox Christian theology, this is the penultimate moment before salvation itself is wrought: 'And some of the bystanders hearing it said, "Behold, he is calling Elijah." And one ran and, filling a sponge full of vinegar, put it on a reed and gave it to him to drink, saying, "Wait, let us see whether Elijah will come to take him down." And Jesus uttered a loud cry, and breathed his last.' It is ironic, or perhaps inevitable, that at the very moment that meaningfulness and meaninglessness become fused in this way, there is a misunderstanding of Christ's words. The last words of Jesus in St. John's Gospel carry the same ambiguity. 'It is finished' can mean either fulfilment of task or termination of life. St. Luke goes for the more straightforward, and one might think heroic, 'Into your hands I commend my spirit'. We should here give close attention to the teaching of the Fathers of Chalcedon. They were insistent that although he was one person, Christ had two natures. Meaningfulness and meaninglessness, the sacred and the secular are to be maintained in their integrity. They are like a rope made of two strands twisted together so hard that they become indistinguishable, and work the same effects together.

For a Christian priest, the cross is the starting point for spirituality. As a priest, I am called to be, expected to be a person of prayer. On the day of ordination, the Bishop asked this question: 'Will you devote yourself to prayer and study, that you may grow in the knowledge and love of God in Jesus Christ?' Whereas I undertook *by God's help* to order my family life in accordance with the teachings of Christ, the response to this question did not carry that rider. It was a simple 'I will'. Priesthood without prayer would have lost its centre, would be fundamentally flawed. Michael Ramsey spoke in his classic work *The Christian Priest Today*:

> the priest, in the Church and for the Church, is the *man of prayer*. Do not all Christians pray? They do indeed, and from many of them we priests can learn to pray and to pray better. Yet 'man [sic] of prayer' is in a special way the role of the priest, and because it is so the Church's prayer will be the stronger. [...] As absolver and pastor, no less than as theologian and teacher, the priest has a prayer which focuses the Church's prayer. In him the Church's prayer is expressed in strength, and it thereby becomes the stronger.[15]

Thus a number of questions arise:

- How is one to be a person of prayer in the midst of an experience of meaninglessness?

- How is one's prayer life transformed in a continuing way by that experience?

---

15   Ramsey (1987), p. 9.

Misunderstanding about prayer lies, one may suspect, at the very root of the Church's relationship with twenty-first century society. I know that there are Christians who do, but I have never believed in a God who intervenes directly in the operations of His universe, in response to prayer faithfully offered. As a priest, I have seen people in great, almost or actually unbearable pain. I cannot believe that God intervenes to save some from pain because they themselves or those who care for them offer especially faithful prayer, or that God would reject prayer that did not have that faithful intensity. The Christian community should not claim for itself any special privileges in relation to human suffering any more than Christ himself was able to do upon the Cross. I believe in a God of supreme goodness: a God of such goodness would forfeit it if he was to intervene in the world in the arbitrary ways that some suspect he does. This is not however to assert a belief in a God who is distant from history. The doctrine of the Incarnation suggests that God's story is woven around our own story. The Creed tell the story of the created world from beginning – 'I believe in God the Father Almighty, creator of heaven and earth' – to the end – 'we look for the resurrection of the dead and life of the world to come' – as it were God's own story. However, not much of this touches popular thinking outside the Church. For many, they see no evidence that God intervenes in his universe, and a lot of evidence that he does not. They therefore conclude that prayer does not work. In a busy modern world which is so largely based on effective and prompt delivery, they come to believe that membership of the Christian community does not make a practical difference.

Thus we need to think, and pray, quite carefully about our theology of prayer. What follows is directed, alongside other readers, at those who have undergone the most difficult experiences, and tries to indicate why I am still a priest, and, I would like to think, a person of prayer. As a priest I am an intercessor, I do pray for people, and with especial love and care for the communities in which I try to serve. The danger of intercessory prayer is that we become suitors at the divine court, making our demands upon God. There is a phase in young people's development when they see the parent simply as the provider: 'I want...' As that relationship grows to maturity, if things go well, the child stops treating the parent as having entered into an alliance for mutual benefit, and simply engages in mutual reciprocity. At their best things are not conditional. As our prayer life matures, we learn that it is about relationship within God, rather than making, often emergency, demands upon God. Thus, in prayer, I have often brought Adam to God, but I have never prayed to God for Adam's healing. This is partly because, for reasons that I have already given, I do not make that kind of request of God, for God does not, and should not, intervene in the world in that way. Even more than that I believe that such a prayer would violate Adam's integrity as a person with autism. I am aware of the expressed reactions of people with disabilities to the prospect of their own healing. Thus, for example, Nancy Eiesland talks about the liturgical laying on of hands, a practice which 'has been closely associated with ritual healing. I, like many people with disabilities have experienced the negative effects of healing rituals. Healing has been the churchly parallel to rehabilitative medicine, in which the goal was "normalization" of the bodies of people with disabilities'.[16]

This way of prayer, this way of 'not interceding' has a deep consistency with the tradition of Christian mysticism. At a certain level of contemplation, one attains a State in which one wants nothing other than God himself. This is well described in the anonymous medieval tract *The Cloud of Unknowing*:

> and if any thought rise and will press continually above thee betwixt thee and that darkness, and ask thee saying, 'What seekest thou, and what wouldest thou have?' say thou, that it is God that thou wouldest have. 'Him I covet, Him I seek, and naught but Him.'[17]

With appropriate spiritual humility, I cannot say whether I have ever attained such a place, but I know that if I did, I would be in a place close to where Adam is. Adam in one way, because of his autistic obsessions, wants everything, but particularly wires, tubes, and pipes. In another way, he wants nothing. All those wants which we in the 'mainstream' of society have – a good income, car, holiday and so on – are beyond his apprehension. For many of us, the ascent of that ladder of contemplation which puts aside our wanting is an arduous task.

---

16   Eiesland (1994), p. 117.
17   Chapter 7, http://www.ccel.org/ccel/anonymous2/cloud.txt [accessed 15 August 2009].

Adam is, at least in some ways, further upon it. There is moreover, beyond the place which I have described, another place, where, in the presence of God, the wanting completely ceases, even the wanting of God. One is then, before God. It is that place which most nearly corresponds to the profound ambiguity of the experience of caring for Adam, where meaning and meaninglessness, what we want, and what we do not want, become fused.

My reliance is upon silence. I find that in times of silence I am living most in solidarity with Adam, in his largely non-verbal world. That is where I want to be, where I long to be. A few days before writing this, I had the tremendous privilege of standing at the back of the chapel of a local Cistercian House, and observing one of the sisters in silent prayer. It was for her a way of life; it was for me a snatched moment of silence. Silence is peace; silence is what happens when things are so difficult that language, its capacity to express what is, breaks apart. Silence does justice to the simultaneous peace and pain of the truly appalling. In silence, we stand at the boundary of the sacred and the secular. The French philosopher Michel Foucault[18] did not have a recognizable prayer life. However, his thinking deals with that which remains unsaid when a discourse is framed, with those who are excluded by powerful discourses. In a late interview in 1983 he was more than usually self-revelatory, talking about the silences of his childhood in bourgeois Poitiers, and then giving his response to the question: *'There is in North-American Indian culture a much greater appreciation of silence than in English-speaking societies, and I suppose in French-speaking societies as well?'*

> Yes, you see, I think silence is one of those things that has been unfortunately dropped from our culture. We don't have a culture of silence […] Young Romans or young Greeks were taught to keep silent in very different ways according to the people with whom they were interacting. Silence was then a specific form of experiencing a relationship with others. This is something that I believe is really worthwhile cultivating. I'm in favour of developing silence as a cultural ethos.[19]

---

18   The subject of my postgraduate research.
19   Foucault (1988), p. 4.

In my calling as a parent and as a priest, I found myself deeply engaged with two worlds: the sacred and the secular. In the exaltation of a culture of silence, I believe that it becomes possible to function within both worlds, without the tension between the two tearing the individual who is trying to function within the two, into two. In any case, I have certainly needed to use silence as a way, perhaps the only way, of experiencing my relationship with my son.

The fountain head of silence is the life of the cloister. Whether one or not one affirms monastic vocation, there is a certain wonder in places where silence rather than communication is prioritized, and where silence – in contrast to the library or the schoolroom, where it exists for the sake of words – is maintained for its own sake. Margaret A. Winzer in her historical account of 'Disability and society before the eighteenth century' shows how the development of the monastic life in the earliest history of the Church was inclusive of those with disabilities:

> The cloistering of disabled persons seemed a natural outgrowth of the monastic impulse, and, in the context of these dark times, it proved advantageous, as it protected them from the dangers confronting them in the general society. A hospice for the blind was established in the fourth century in Caesarea in Cappadocia (in present day Turkey). As the centuries passed, hospices – many offering facilities for other special groups – gradually spread across Europe. [...] Cloistering was not restricted to blind persons. Saint Basil, Bishop of Caesarea in AD 370, gathered all types of disabled people into the monastic institutions that he controlled. Each group had separate quarters, but all engaged in common work and worship. Legend holds that during the same century Nicholas the Bishop of Myra, a town in present day southern Turkey provided dowries for poor girls and cared for idiots and imbeciles.[20]

This is not to idealize the attitudes of early and medieval Catholicism to those with disabilities. It is simply to observe that people with disabilities found their place within communities of prayer. One could imagine that for a person with autism the high levels of structure within the daily monastic regime, the provision within that daily routine of productive work alongside the removal of the constant need to communicate with others could prove highly beneficial. The modern

---

20   In Davis (ed.) (1997), pp. 89–90.

period saw the development of institutions specifically for those with learning disabilities and mental health problems. There is some evidence that the middle ages had come to provide that dedicated institutional environment, without the exclusionary stigma that it was *for* those with learning disabilities and mental health problems. The purpose of the cloister was quite other.

If silence is the way to God, we need to reflect then upon the God to whom we pray, whose company we keep in the silence. The question to be asked is the extent to which, and the way in which we can be said to 'know God'. St. Paul in the first letter to the Corinthians tells that 'since, in the wisdom of God, the world did not know God through wisdom, it pleased God through the folly of what we preach to save those who believe'.[21] It is axiomatic that, in relation to the mystery of God, we all have a cognitive deficit: it is not through wisdom that we know God. In this passage, Paul speaks of 'eloquent wisdom', he correlates cognitive ability and speech, but stresses their intrinsic limitation: 'Where is the wise man? Where is the scribe? Where is the debater of this age? Has not God made foolish the wisdom of the world?' Paul's anthropology, his description of what it is to be human, has a mirror image in his theology: 'For the foolishness of God is wiser than men, and the weakness of God is stronger than men.' God's wisdom is such that it includes 'foolishness': it transcends the distinction between cognitive ability and cognitive deficit, and is thus able to transcend the divine–human distinction.

This leads us to the traditional question of 'the analogy of being', *analogia entis*. The classic statement of this comes from the second canon of the Fourth Lateran Council in 1215. As part of a wider argument to condemn Joachim of Fiore in his questioning of the Trinitarian teachings of Peter Lombard, the Council cited as a proof text Matthew 5:48, 'Be perfect as your heavenly Father is perfect', construing this as a reference to the perfection by grace of humanity, likened but contrasted to the perfection by nature of God, and continued: 'Between the Creator and the creature so great a likeness cannot be noted without the necessity of noting a greater dissimilarity between them.'[22] In order for us as human beings to know any thing which is, it has to

---

21   1 Corinthians 1:21.
22   Cited in Moltmann (2000), p. 155.

be on the one hand distinct from us, dissimilar to us, and yet, also in order to be known it has to be of sufficient similarity to us that we can perceive it. One is always mindful of the dangers in any talk about the existence of God of making God a thing in his own universe alongside other things, but it can be plausibly suggested that our knowledge of other things is rooted upon our knowledge of God, and that it has its character taken from the way in which we know God. We know things in this particular way, because this is the way that we know the Creator of all things. The consequence of this is that similarity and difference are both at the heart of all being, and characterize our relationship with God. We tend to think of difference, as being, by its very nature, marginal – it may well be central. Whenever we reflect upon Adam, and the nature of his difference, we may be near to something of more than marginal significance. It is thus ironic that the Fathers of the Fourth Lateran Council condemned Joachim of Fiore – and what is at stake here is not, as it was in 1215, the correctness or otherwise of his teachings – as 'heretic and insane'.

The *analogia entis* has its critics: the theology of Karl Barth had a programmatic commitment to refuting the *analogia entis* in favour of the *analogia fidei*. It is of a piece with his theology of revelation, which insists on the primacy of revelation, of God's grace from above, rather than human understanding working by analogy and taking the initiative from below. The danger of such a theology of revelation is that it takes up the language of divine perfection, and treats grace as the imposing of divine perfection upon humanity. The dangers from the point of view of the spirituality which we are here attempting to construct are manifold: if we take God as omnipotent, omniscient, all-loving, and then define humanity as falling short of these perfections, divine grace becomes another element in the apparatus of normalization which is all too familiar to people with disabilities and their carers. Indeed it becomes part of the medicalized model of disability. Grace is the way to salvation; salvation can be, as Tillich suggests, from its root in the Latin *salvus* interpreted as 'healing'.[23]

However, there is another way of reflecting upon the classic Protestant schema of salvation, of which Karl Barth's thinking is a part. Within this schema, the total capacity for salvation belongs

---

23   Tillich (ed.) (1978), p. 166.

to God. In ways which are very much in agreement with his own Protestant heritage, Tillich examines ways of self-salvation, through moral legalism, through asceticism, through mysticism, through sacraments, through doctrines, through emotional response. In turn, he outlines the failure to achieve what they set out to do. The history of religion, he argues, is, to an extent, 'the history of man's attempts and failures to save himself'.[24] On this account, the capacity remains with God; the incapacity with humanity. Thus rather than seeing disability as belonging to a certain group within humanity, it belongs to all. The problem is when we see grace as overcoming our human disability, and of bringing salvation and healing to some. This problem occurs within the classic schema, when revelation, the capacity of God to save us, becomes distorted into self-salvation: 'On the basis of revelatory experiences, religion turns to self-salvation. It distorts what it has received, and fails in what it tries to achieve. This is the tragedy of religion.' Moreover, Tillich believes that there is that which transcends divine capacity and human disability, with an explicit criticism of Barth's views: 'It is equally wrong to identify religion with revelation, just as it is wrong to identify religion with the attempt at self-salvation. Religion like all life is ambiguous...'

Within philosophy of religion, there is one strand that seeks to apply a strict logic to religious thought. It takes strict logic as a means of overcoming, of thinking out, the ambiguities of religion and life. Over 30 years ago, Richard Swinburne produced a much reprinted volume, *The Coherence of Theism*. Before showing in further detail how this fits into the discussion here, it is worth looking at the two elements of the title. Swinburne's sense of the deity, at least as his starting point, reflects some of the problems to which we have already referred.

> By a theist I understand a man [sic] who believes that there is a God. By a 'God' he understands something like 'a person without a body (i.e. a spirit) who is eternal, free, able to do anything, knows everything, is perfectly good, is the proper object of human worship and obedience, the creator and sustainer of the universe'.

---

24   Ibid., pp. 80–86.

God is understood as totally abled, and thus stands in cosmic contrast with those who are disabled. Coherence for Swinburne is the avoidance in a given statement of internal contradiction. The conditions for coherence, and thence for the coherence of theism, are strict and logical; 'Given that a certain sentence expresses a statement, makes a claim, what further must be the case if it is to express a coherent claim?' As he has already shown in a previous chapter, 'if a statement expresses an incoherent supposition, it will entail a self-contradictory statement – which henceforth I will call, simply, a contradiction. The statement expresses an incoherent supposition, for buried in it is a claim that a thing is so and that it is not so. It follows that if a statement does not entail any contradiction, then it expresses a coherent supposition.' If Swinburne's God, who one would acknowledge is the God of many more people than Swinburne himself, is in His very nature exclusionary, then the way in which Swinburne reflects upon Him is exclusionary too. I have never found such strict logic appealing, but I was always a little afraid that in all its baffling complexity, it just might be right, even though strict logic has taken as many people from God as to Him. Logic is by its very nature dogmatic, any claim that it makes is 'without contradiction'. While recognizing the many virtues of such an approach, life with Adam would convince almost (I suspect) anybody – that other ways to God have to sit alongside it.

However, when Swinburne turns to the question of divine omnipotence, which, we can allow, is the most difficult of the classic divine attributes for a person with disabilities, then something of great interest occurs. It is not my intention here to offer a complete discussion of the paradox, which Swinburne undertakes with great technical skill and aplomb, with a great personal capacity in the use of reason, but merely to record the initial problem which he confronts.

> The paradox arises when we ask whether God, allegedly an omnipotent being, can make a stone too heavy for himself to lift. If he cannot, the argument goes, then there is an action which God cannot perform, viz. make such a stone. If he can, then there will be a different action which he cannot perform viz. lift the stone. Either way, the argument goes, there is an action which God cannot perform, and so [...] he is not omnipotent. What applies to God applies to any other being, and so, the argument goes, it is not coherent to suppose that there be an omnipotent being.

If we go back behind Swinburne's analysis to the original paradox, the suggestion is that omnipotence carries with it an inbuilt self-limitation. The omnipotent capacity to do things comprises within itself incapacity. There is that which transcends ability and disability.

There is however another version of the paradox of the stone which would substitute for the stone too hard to lift, a puzzle, an intellectual challenge too hard for God to resolve. It could be suggested that God has already done this: He has created a puzzle too hard for Him to solve, and that is the creation itself. God Himself, as all-knowing, has to know what it is to be beyond the limit of His cognitive ability. If God is puzzled, then we should not be surprised to be so too. Again, those with disabilities are not on the margins, but at the heart of creation.

Although the line of approach suggested by Swinburne is, as I have suggested, potentially fruitful, it is not there that my theology landed. The paradox which he here considers arises from his concept of God. I would want to suggest, in keeping with the tradition of Christian mysticism, that there is a God beyond that God. In the volume, *Silence and the Word – negative theology and incarnation*, edited by Oliver Davies and Denys Turner, a number of distinguished theologians turn their attention to the question of what is called 'apophatic' theology. As the preface indicates, there was a consensus between the contributors that 'the dimension of negativity, or *apophasis*, which is most often associated with the canon of Christian mystical texts, belongs also to mainstream Christianity and can be found in theological works not normally considered to be of a "mystical" kind'. It is programmatic for the argument of this book that mysticism and spirituality cannot be allowed to remain on the margins of the life of the Church, but should fill the life of the Church, and thence be enabled to occupy the border between the sacred and the secular. The approach contrasts with that of Swinburne – of making positive statements about God, which can then be scrutinized for their coherence. Rather, we proceed by saying what God is not, and show that He is beyond all human categories. In his introductory contribution to the volume *Apophaticism, Idolatry and the Claims of Reason*, Denys Turner gives a lengthly quotation from the sermons of Meister Eckhart. It shows with great clarity the way of proceeding of apophatic theology, and needs to be reproduced at length to give it its full impact. It should be noted that Eckhart in his lifetime was tried for heresy, and that in 1329, around the time of his death, a Papal Bull, *In agro dominico*, stigmatized his teachings.

> God is nameless, because no-one can say anything or understand anything about him. Therefore a pagan teacher says: 'Whatever we understand or say about the First Cause, that it is far more ourselves than it is the First Cause, for it is beyond all saying and understanding.' So, if I say, 'God is good',[25] that is not true. I am good but God is not good. I can even say: 'I am better than God', for whatever is good can become better and whatever can become better can become best of all. But since God is not good, he cannot become better. And since he cannot become better, he cannot be best of all. For these three degrees are alien to God: 'good', 'better' and best, for he is superior to them all... If I say 'God is a being' it is not true; he is a being transcending being and [he is] transcending nothingness... [So] do not try to understand God, for God is beyond all understanding. One authority says: 'If I had a God whom I could understand, I should never consider him God'.[26] If you can understand anything about him, it in no way belongs to him, and insofar as you understand anything about him that brings you into incomprehension, and from incomprehension you are arrive at a brute's stupidity... So if you do not wish to be brutish, do not understand God who is beyond words.[27]

Adam cannot give God a name. He cannot say anything about him. To be the best of our knowledge, he cannot understand God. That is a condition which – following Eckhart – he shares with the human race. When, as a result of life with Adam, I wrestled with issues to do with creation, I should have realized that the 'First Cause' is beyond all saying and understanding. We will see later, when we examine the Book of Job, that the natural human response to human difficulty is to seek to evaluate God. Natural response it may be; but it is not the right place to start: for God stands beyond our human values and evaluation, beyond our 'good', 'better' and 'best'. Lest it be thought that to say

---

25   Taken, as Turner notes, from Liber de Causis. Turner and Davies (eds.) (1999), p 12. The Liber de Causis was a Aristotelian treatise based on an Arabic original.

26   Turner notes these as a rough paraphrase of words by St. Augustine. Ibid., p. 12.

27   Cited at ibid. pp. 12–13. Original text taken from Sermon 83, *Meister Eckhart: the essential sermons, commentaries, treatises and defense* (trans. and introd. Edmund Colledge and Bernard McGinn, New York: Paulist Press, 1981).

with Eckhart that God is not good dethrones him from His Godhead, we note that God is 'superior' to all those values. Eckhart opened here for me some way of responding to the question of whether Adam is a blessing from God – 'Has God been good in all of this?' – by allowing the whole range of responses, all of the responses. To the extent that someone in a similar situation might question the very existence of God, Eckhart shows God himself as being beyond that question, beyond being. The natural response to Adam's situation is to try to understand: Eckhart's injunction is that we should not try to understand God. I should not; Adam cannot. In different ways, we are letting God be God.

CHAPTER 4

Autism and Identity

There is a famous poem in the Welsh language by Waldo Williams, *Brawdoliaeth* [Brotherhood], from which this is taken:

'Mae rhwydwaith dirgel Duw
yn cydio pob dyn byw;
Cymod a chyflawn we
Myfi, Tydi, Efe...'

'God's mysterious net
Binds every living person;
Reconciliation and the whole web
Of Me, You, Him...'

Whether like Waldo one roots it in a deity, we take for granted that social world, the world of individuals, relationships and groups. It is the network on which the sphere of the public and the private is predicated. For Adam, this world does not exist: he is in it, yet not of it.

Historians have sought to trace the rise of Western individualism, and have located it within different historical eras. It could be argued that the Western Catholic Church represented a high point of a collective sense of being overwhelming any sense of individuality: people did not speak of individuality because they did not have a language for its expression. Jacob Burckhardt in his classic work *The Civilisation of the Renaissance in Italy* suggested that:

In the Middle Ages both sides of human consciousness– that which was turned within as that which was turned without – lay dreaming or half awake beneath a common veil. The veil was woven of faith, illusion and childish prepossession, through which the world and history were seen clad in strange hues. Man [sic] was conscious of himself only as a member of a race, people, party, family or corporation – only through some general category.'[1]

It could be argued that this way of being began to be overtaken by something quite different at some time before the close of the middle ages. Some scholars place it early. Colin Morris in his *Discovery of the Individual* writes of the period between 1050 and 1200. Burckhardt himself believed that 'at the close of the thirteenth century, Italy began to swarm with individuality; the ban laid upon human personality was dissolved; and a thousand figures meet us each in its own special shape and dress'.[2] The era of humanism brought a turn from a society constituted by the worship of God to the celebration of humanity and the potential of individual human achievement. In literature there was a new interest in biography; in art an interest in individual physiognomy.

It can be argued that Luther's Reformation arose from the culture of Renaissance humanism; that Renaissance humanism created the conditions for the Reformation to take place. In *The Cambridge Companion to Reformation Theology* Scott Hendrix discusses what he calls the 'Reformation discovery', the insight within which the elements of 'what would become a new theology' are found:

> According to Luther's own account, the discovery was a biblical and theological insight that solved a religious and exegetical problem. He could not understand how Paul could say that the righteousness of God was revealed in the gospel (Romans 1:16-17), when he had been taught to understand divine righteousness as the basis on which God punished unrighteous sinners. Despite his own irreproachable life as a monk, Luther says he hated this righteous God because God seemed to be adding the Gospel with its threat of punishment to the burden of the law. After persistent study and meditation, however, he suddenly understood from the full text of Romans 1:17 that 'the person who through faith is righteous shall live', and that accordingly the righteousness of God revealed in the gospel was the passive righteousness through which God justifies

---

1   1990, p. 98.
2   Idem.

us by faith. 'Here I felt that I was altogether born again, and had entered paradise through open gates.'[3]

Historians have struggled to fit Luther's much later account of his *Turberlebnis* [tower experience] into the known chronology of his career.[4] There is however a danger in taking his account of it at face value: it is in the nature of the experience for him to experience it as new, as new insight, new discovery. The experience as described is that of personal conversion, the template from which so many personal conversion narratives within the Protestant tradition have been shaped. It is predicated upon the idea that the salvation of the individual as individual is important. By the beginning of the sixteenth century the importance of the individual was far from being a new idea. Moreover, in Luther's account, the experience is one of divinely inspired cognition: 'after persistent study' as well as meditation, 'he suddenly understood that…' Although Luther would cast the matter as that of divine grace, rather than salvation by works – including those of study – we are here not at all far from the humanist idea of human capacity, of the achieving intellect. To say that the Lutheran (and post-Lutheran) conversion experience is simply the sacralization of an experience within secular culture of the (post humanist) rise of the individual is in no way to minimize its significance.

What is offered here is more than an exercise in historical reconstruction. The Protestant Reformation and the Renaissance have shaped modern culture and experience in ways of which we are now – from day to day – barely conscious. The exaltation of the achieving individual is at the centre of our modern culture. Insofar as it is recognized spiritual life is perceived in the same way, so that an individual makes a choice from a range of belief systems, using as a criterion the extent to which the choice made will contribute most fully to that individual's personal flourishing. It is no reflection upon the glories of Renaissance culture or upon the spiritual achievement of the Reformation to say that they have jointly created a public sphere from which those who are not able to achieve, and whose very way of being runs counter to the exaltation of the individual and the personal, are

---

3   Bagchi and Steinmetz (2004), p. 42.
4   MacCulloch (2003), pp. 118–119.

excluded. We need therefore to take the story forward, to see if there is anything within the subsequent development of Western thinking about the individual which has either enhanced or held in question the patterns established at the time of the Renaissance and Reformation.

By the seventeenth century we find another kind of individualism at the root of Cartesian rationalism. The starting point of Descartes' philosophy is radical scepticism, doubting even the existence of the visible everyday world. Having taken doubt to its limit, he asks if there is anything left:

> And observing that this truth 'I am thinking, therefore I exist' [famously, *cogito ergo sum*] was so firm and sure that all the most extravagant suppositions of the skeptics were incapable of shaking it, I decided that I could accept it without scruple as the first principle of the philosophy I was seeking.[5]

It is on the basis of the irreducible thinking, rational, logical – 'therefore' – subjectivity, the 'I', that the tradition of the eighteenth-century Enlightenment is at least partly built. Having reduced everything to the *cogito*, Descartes expands from the *cogito* so that the rational self rationally considers, rationally experiences the world around him or her. This can be correlated with one particular interpretation of the autistic spectrum. Stuart Powell and Rita Jordan in their article 'Being objective about autistic thinking and learning to learn' present 'their notion that a key problem in autism is that the individual fails to develop a sense of "experiencing self". This would lead to a fragmentation of experiences because there would be no sense of self to link these experiences.'[6] This is the specific challenge which autism presents to the *cogito*, but there is a wider challenge from irrationality in general to the Enlightenment project of the exaltation of reason. As Descartes had built his philosophy upon the self-intuiting, rational individual, so the life of society had to be built upon that same foundation: society would thus be built upon rationality recognizing itself in others. The problem came when what rationality recognized in some other was irrationality. In his work first published in 1961, *Histoire de la Folie à l'âge classique* [History of Madness in the Age of

---

5   Descartes (1968), pp. 53–54.
6   The quotation is taken from Morgan, (1996), p. 117. The original article is in *Educational Psychology*, 13, 359–370.

Reason] Michel Foucault gives us one account of what happened in these circumstances. It should be stressed that it is only one account which has since been subject to strong critical scrutiny by historians, including Roy Porter.[7] Foucault's focus, however, is upon one particular event in French history, the royal edict of 26 April 1656 which led to the creation of the general hospital in Paris. Foucault describes the processes by which 'the mad', those whom we would describe as having mental health problems, from occupying a marginal position on the very edges of medieval society, became the targets of 'le grand renfermement', the great confinement. As time went past, outside the great urban communities, the great Victorian asylums were to be built as part of this continuing history. Foucault speaks of the disciplinary discourses which were formed in this period, such as psychiatry, psychology, criminology, by which individual human subjectivity came to be described and indeed constituted.

In the 1960s, the decade to which Foucault's first major published work belonged, things changed. In the United Kingdom, a major policy shift was initiated by Enoch Powell's water tower speech of 1961, towards the closure of the old county asylums, and the relocation of many of those with mental health problems to wards attached to general hospitals. On a more global scale, the 1960s saw the flowering of the anti-psychiatry movement including many figures of whom R.D. Laing is possibly the most well known. Foucault responded to this intellectual climate by suggesting that the human subject as constituted by the humanistic discourses of previous centuries may well be coming to an end. In the famous concluding passage to *Les Mots et les Choses [The Order of Things]* in 1966, the year before David Cooper published his *Psychiatry and Anti-Psychiatry*, Foucault wrote that 'Man [sic, l'homme] is an invention of which the archaeology of thought easily shows the recent date. And perhaps the nearness of his end.' The very last words of the book speak of man being effaced 'like a face of sand on the edge of the sea'.[8]

---

7   See Porter (2006), pp. 17–22 for a critical evaluation of what Porter for all his
    professional scepticism is willing to admit is 'this powerful and highly influential
    interpretation'.

8   *Les Mots et les Choses*, p. 398.

Foucault's thinking about the death of the subject is of a piece with other thinking, contemporary to him, about the death of the author. In *The Death of the Author* Roland Barthes sought to show how the very figure of the author arose from the context of Western culture which we have already been considering:

> The author is a modern figure, a product of our society insofar as, emerging from the Middle Ages with English empiricism, French rationalism and the personal faith of the Reformation, it discovered the prestige of the individual, of, as it is more nobly put, the 'human person'. It is thus logical that in literature it should be this positivism, the epitome and culmination of capitalist ideology, which has attached the greatest importance to the 'person' of the author. The *author* still reigns in histories of literature, biographies of writers, interviews, magazines, as in the consciousness of men [sic] of letters anxious to unite their person and their work through diaries and memoires. The image of literature to be found in ordinary culture is tyrannically centred on the author, his person, his life, his tastes, his passions… […] The *explanation* of the work is always sought in the man or woman who produced it…"[9]

Having described the rise of the author, Barthes in the remainder of the piece makes a number of moves. He throws our attention from the author to the text. Thus, for example, 'Mallarmé's entire poetics consists in suppressing the author in the interests of writing.'[10] In turn, the text does not have a fixed meaning, predetermined by authorial intention: '…literature, by refusing to assign a "secret", an ultimate meaning, to the text (and to the world as text), liberates what may be called an anti-theological activity, an activity that is truly revolutionary since to refuse to fix meaning is, in the end, to refuse God and his hypostases – reason, science, law'.[11] By refusing a single coherent meaning to the text, Barthes is enabled to transfer the focus from the author, via the text to the reader: 'The reader is the space on which all the quotations that make up a writing are inscribed without any of them being lost; a text's unity lies not in its origin but in its destination.'[12]

---

9   Burke (1995), pp. 124–125. Barthes' 'Death of the author' is given in full, pp. 124–130.
10   Ibid., p. 126.
11   Ibid., p. 129.
12   Ibid., p. 129.

It is in Barthes' thinking that I can begin to see some way out of the impasse of Adam's way of being caught – entrapped, one might say – within the post-medieval frameworks of Western culture. Adam is not able to be an author. He is, as Michel Foucault put it, drawing upon the thought of his friend Barthes, *sans œuvre*. For Barthes, the author as a productive person was one element in the whole structure of Western capitalism. Adam will not produce text; he will not take his place within that structure. His very way of being radically eschews authorship. Yet in another way he has been radically productive of a very diverse discourse, of which this book is a part, but also, *inter alia*, includes the reports of psychologists, individual educational plans, social services assessments and even television documentaries. Through this book, I have reflected upon that collection of discourses: as we have seen, and as we will see, I would refuse to ascribe to it, or impose upon it one single and coherent meaning. I would seek to transfer the focus from the author and the text to the reader her/himself, and that would be you.

At the end of Chapter 3, I suggested that Adam's 'condition' tells us something about the human 'condition' in relationship to God. In this chapter, I have suggested that autism as a 'condition' can give us important insights into the way in which – over the long term – our human thinking about our own individuality has developed. I am now going to attempt, briefly, to take that one stage further. We have already seen, again at the end of Chapter 3, the particular insights which a negative, apophatic theology can give us. In such a theology, the stress is not so much on the positive statements which we can make about God, but upon the negatives, upon what God is not. I would have a natural reluctance to map the structure of an account of the Godhead, a theology, onto the structure of an account of humanity, an anthropology. However, I do believe that this is a move which is opened up for us by a doctrine of the Incarnation. As an orthodox Christian, if I want to have a sense of what divinity/humanity is, I look at Jesus. The Incarnation opens up the possibility of building upon a negative theology to create a negative anthropology. As we have seen, the divine attributes build up an image of an able God. As Fénelon called him: 'the God of the attributes' – 'power, wisdom, goodness, and the like'.[13] Just as I am more impressed by the God about whom I cannot, and should not, speak, so I am beginning to think – with some irony in the centre of a book which is all about Adam – that what is important about him is that which we cannot say about him. His diagnosis – following DSM IV[14] – represents an attempt to place him within the categories of our able society. I would suggest that Adam's actual identity, like that of all disabled people, transcends his diagnosis. If it is possible to take this strategy in relating to Adam, it may well be possible to do so with humanity in general. Instead of looking, as we do within the humanist tradition of Western thought, for the individual and collective attributes of humanity, it may well be that we would be better to look for what humanity is not, rather than what it is. One of the advantages of this is that we immediately allow the transcendent, the mystical back into our relations with those with whom we have to do from day to day, while simultaneously affirming secular thinking of the death of the subject, and the death of the author.

There is clearly an enormous contrast between this chapter in the book and Chapter 2 which describes in detail the daily experience of living with Adam. That chapter, although it is to some extent shaped by my own interpretation, is in one sense uncontroversial – although the same material would be written in different ways by different participants in the events described, there is little room to doubt that that was the way it was, that was how it seemed from the perspective of one of those most closely involved. In contrast, this chapter is full of controversy within a short space: there are many who would want to challenge the interpretations offered of the Renaissance, Reformation, Enlightenment and modern literary theory. However, I suspect that more important than all those questions is how we link up the grand historical and literary issues with the simple givens of everyday life. It might be suggested, even if the account of the Western tradition given here is accepted as being close to what was the case, that the great events in the history of thought are too large, too intractable, too historically given to be of concern to us. However, it is the case that Adam, alongside others with autism, or with other disabilities,

13   Maxims of the Saints: http://www.ccel.org/f/fenelon/maxims/maxims.htm [accessed 15 August 2009].
14   Diagnostic and Statistical Manual of Mental Disorders. See p. 24.

meets from day to day people whose world of thought – usually subconsciously – has been totally determined by a combination of our cultural tradition and contemporary thinking. I have tried to show how that tradition is disabling, and how some contemporary thinking allows escape routes from all of that. It is only when we follow those routes that we will be able to distinguish between that which – external to him – disables him, and that which belongs to his disability. Once reduced in that way, it will be interesting to see how much disability is left.

CHAPTER 5

Faith and (Un) Reason – Towards A Systematic Theology

We have seen at the end of the previous chapter that theology may well have to be simultaneously counter-cultural in regard to history, and working with the grain of culture in regard to contemporary thought. In this chapter we will consider in detail the nuances of the relationship between faith and philosophy. One option for Christians down the ages has been to turn against rational philosophy, or indeed any kind of philosophy. The argument between faith and reason is not simply a modern controversy, dating back only to the aftershock of the eighteenth-century Enlightenment. The classic statement of this is from Tertullian (c. 165–225), a view that there is nothing more needed than Christian faith in its simplicity:

> What indeed has Athens to do with Jerusalem? What concord is there between the Academy and the Church? what between heretics and Christians? Our instruction comes from 'the porch of Solomon,' who had himself taught that 'the Lord should be sought in simplicity of heart.' [Wisdom 1:1] Away with all attempts to produce a mottled Christianity of Stoic, Platonic, and dialectic composition! We want no curious disputation after possessing Christ Jesus, no inquisition after enjoying the gospel! With our faith, we desire no further belief. For this is our palmary [victorious, worthy

to bear the palm] faith, that there is nothing which we ought to believe besides.[1]

This triumphalist account of faith has had many echoes down the centuries, in any form of Christianity which deliberately turns its back upon contemporary intellectual and cultural context, whatever that context may be at any given time. In its entirety this book is about the challenge which the care of a person with autism has brought to faith. I would share with Tertullian a sense that there are specific Christian insights which can be brought to bear on any human experience. However, under the pressure of that experience, I found myself moving beyond faith, to explore the road which leads from theology to philosophy. I have already spoken of the way in which I was compelled to live beyond the sacred and the secular. In order to live in that space, theology on its own was not sufficient to my psychological and indeed intellectual needs. The basis of all this can be found in Scripture, and especially in the famous prologue to the Gospel according to St. John, in the logos theology of that Gospel:

> In the beginning was the Word, and the Word was with God, and the Word was God. He was in the beginning with God; all things were made through him, and without him was not anything made that was made. In him was life, and the life was the light of men... And the Word became flesh and dwelt among us, full of grace and truth; we have beheld his glory, glory as of the only Son from the Father.[2]

The same prologue speaks of John the Baptist's witness to the Christ. It is in Christian witness that the intrinsic connection between theology and philosophy arises. In seeking to describe the Christ event, the writer of the Gospel does not start from within the language and terminology of the Christian community. Rather he takes a term from contemporary Hellenistic culture and philosophy, logos, denoting that which is said, and thence, by extension, reason. St. John the Evangelist implicitly addresses that Hellenistic audience with the claim that if you use, and indeed have grasped, the term logos, you have access to that which belongs to the Christian mystery of salvation.

---

1   Tertullian De Praescriptione Hereticorum, Chapter 7, 9–13.

2   John 1:1-3, 14.

Once one has established the basic principle that in the process of its formation any Christian systematic theology should be in dialogue with philosophy, there is then a further question to be approached. The pressures of caring for Adam had forced me to look over the boundary from theology to philosophy, to examine the nexus between theology and philosophy. However, the question then arose as to which philosophy, and as to the criteria by which such a choice should be made. Should theology's choice of philosophical dialogue partner be based on simple theological criteria, choosing that philosophy from within the range of choices available in any historical period which is most congenial to theology? Should theology's choice be made on strictly philosophical grounds, so that the choice is made without theological presuppositions, and so that theology has to respond to any of the tough demands which a philosophy so chosen makes upon it? The specific and intensely personal challenge which I faced as a theologian was that my knowledge of Adam led me to a view that he held up a challenge to many of the available philosophical options, as well as affirming some others.

Of these options, I shall now present a selection. This cannot be an exhaustive account, but the selection that I present gives an indication of the depths of that challenge. I approach all the philosophical systems to which I refer with a due sense of humility. At the root of the Christian tradition, we find Christian Platonism. The depths of that root are so far down that Nietzsche's polemic could describe Christianity in the preface to *Beyond Good and Evil* as 'Platonism for the people'. Nietzsche distrusted Platonism, Christianity, and indeed very possibly the people. A turn towards Platonism had allowed Christianity to establish its credibility within the late classical world. Pre-eminent among those early theologians with strong Platonic influence upon them was Augustine. In Book 8, Chapter 5 of *The City of God*, Augustine asks the question: 'If Plato says that the wise man is the man who imitates, knows and loves this God, and that participation in this God brings man [sic] happiness, what need is there to examine other philosophers?' He responds to his own question with the assertion that 'there are none who come nearer to us than the Platonists'.[3] An Augustinian thread runs through the subsequent

---

3   Augustine (1972 trans.), p. 304.

history of theology through Luther and beyond. A discussion of the appeal of Platonism to these early Christian writers is beyond the scope of this book. However, we can identify from Augustine the appeal of Platonism's postulation of an invisible realm beyond the immediate and the material, an eternal realm in which humanity subject to change and decay has the opportunity to participate. In Chapter 6 of the same book, Augustine tells us that the Platonists:

> these philosophers, as we have seen, have been raised above the rest by a glorious reputation they so thoroughly deserve; and they recognized that no material object can be God; for that reason they raised their eyes above all material objects in their search for God. They realized that nothing changeable can be the supreme God; and therefore in their search for the supreme God they raised their eyes above all mutable souls and spirits.[4]

One can see the appeal of such ideas. The danger is in a dualism which sets up the spiritual against the physical, the soul against the body, the invisible against the visible, material world and in each case prioritizes the former. It is hard to express in words the sheer physicality of the experience of caring for Adam. That physicality arose partly from his lack of language skills, so that our relationship with him could not be located in the abstract and the transcendent. It arose partly from the simple practicalities of managing his toileting problem. In those circumstances, a turn towards a Platonic philosophy could have been an easy escape. One may suspect that some people at times of difficulty turn to Christianity, when what is actually appealing to them – unbeknown to them – is the deep Platonic strain within Christianity. For my part I was concerned about the way in which Platonism calls a spiritual world into existence to redress the painful unbalance of the real. There is a danger that such a spiritual world will provide a place of flight and refuge from facing the bleak realities of life in the immediate world.

There is a further specific difficulty with Platonic thought, and this belongs to the Platonic doctrine of Forms. Commentators are careful to point out that this doctrine undergoes development in the course of Plato's career. We can take from his middle period the comment in

---

4   Ibid., p. 307.

the *Republic* that 'Whenever a name is applied to many different things, there is a form corresponding to the name'.[5] The form of an individual thing exists in the world beyond changeable reality. Within changeable reality, there are, for example, many individual things to which the name 'chair' can be applied. Plato's view is that, beyond changeable reality, and beyond all the individual instances of 'chair', there is an unchangeable ideal form of the 'chair', from which all the individual instances derive. We can take this further, and say that there are many individuals to whom the name 'human' can be applied. Plato would argue that beyond every individual human, there is the idealized form of the human. There are dangers in this for disabled people, in that they can be considered – wrongly – as somehow damaged versions of the transcendent ideal of the human. Preferable to Plato's view is that of Aristotle, whose doctrine of universals does not allow there to be some separable form beyond all the individual instances of a thing or person. In other words, for Aristotle, we arrive at our concept of humanity by considering all the individual instances of humanity, and then framing the universal from those individual instances. In order to arrive at the universal humanity, we need to have considered Adam, and all of those with disabilities, before we formulate our overarching concept of humanity. We will see later on how important this is in our formulation of the human rights of those with disabilities. For the moment it suggests that we should take rationality and speech – which some take to be essential attributes of humanity – as less than essential to our concept of humanity.

I will now move over many centuries in order to examine twentieth-century philosophies. It was perhaps only in the twentieth century that philosophy succeeded in establishing its autonomy from theology. Philosophers no longer necessarily had prior training in theology; their works could be appropriated and, where possible, understood without reference to the sphere of the theological. As philosophy emancipated itself from theology, so also it emancipated itself from the (often unspoken) Platonic roots of classical Christian theological reflections. Whether or not previous philosophers were

---

5   *Republic* 596a. Cited in Kraut (ed.) (1992), p. 8, which also gives a useful summary of the way in which Plato's thinking about the forms developed.

self-acknowledged neo-Platonists, they were nonetheless stuck with the Platonic foundations of theology.

One of the well known features of twentieth-century philosophy is the 'linguistic turn', and within that the pre-eminent place of the thought of Ludwig Wittgenstein. As he was – among many other things – a philosopher of language, I suspected that Wittgenstein might provide me with the resources for reflecting upon life with a individual who is largely non-verbal, and for all practical purposes illiterate. Language seems to be self-evidently what it is: as it belongs so much to the everyday world, we sometimes can be led to avoid the fundamental mystery of the nature of language. The question which I asked in approaching Wittgenstein was 'What is this thing which Adam has not got?' or better, 'What is this thing that Adam barely has?'

On this subject, Wittgenstein's views changed in the course of his career. His associates at Cambridge, including Bertrand Russell, very much belonged to the 'analytic' tradition of philosophy. In the first place, Wittgenstein shared with them a fascination with the ways in which 'ordinary language' can be reduced to a logical structure. This project shares the characteristic of the whole post-Enlightenment project, in that it is – one may say, inadvertently – exclusionary of those who are non-rational, with rationality in this case being taken to the mathematical heights of logical notation. However, it does indicate that there is a profound connection between Adam's lack of rationality and his lack of language. That profound connection is indicated in a very different way by the term of the New Testament, and of ancient Greek philosophy, logos – denoting both speech and reason. This is not the place to even attempt a detailed account of Wittgenstein's philosophical career. However, the *Philosophical Investigations* mark a turning point in his thinking. He begins by citing St. Augustine's personal account of his own language acquisition as a child from the *Confessions*:

> When they called something by name and pointed it out while they spoke, I saw it and realized that the thing they wished to indicate was called by the name they then uttered. And what they meant was made plain by the gestures of their bodies, by a kind of natural language, common to all nations, which expresses itself

through changes of countenance, glances of the eye, gestures and intonations which indicate a disposition and attitude – either to seek or to possess, to reject or to avoid. So it was that by frequently hearing words, in different phrases, I gradually identified the objects which the words stood for and, having formed my mouth to repeat these signs, I was thereby able to express my will.[6]

This passage refers a whole range of things which were at the heart of Adam not acquiring language: his lack of protoactive pointing; his blindness to body language; his unconcern with mimetic behaviour. What Wittgenstein goes on to argue is that the situation which Augustine is describing – word and object corresponding to each other within a strict logic – is not in fact a description of language. Rather it is one language game among others. The term 'language game' famously belongs to Wittgenstein's philosophy. In the *Philosophical Investigations* he gives us an indication of what a language game is: 'I will also call the whole consisting of language and the actions into which it is woven a language game.'[7] The move is from a correspondence theory of language, the correspondence of word and object, to a way of thinking about language which sets it within its social context, and the many different ways in which language is used. P.M.S. Hacker, the great expert on Wittgenstein, described in his *Dictionary of National Biography* article the central development of Wittgenstein's thought from the *Tractatus* to the *Philosophical Investigations*:

Consequently, the central thought of the Tractatus, that any form of representation is answerable to reality, that it must, in its formal structure, mirror the metaphysical form of the world, is misconceived. Concepts are not correct or incorrect, only more or less useful. Rules for the use of words are not true or false. They are answerable neither to reality, nor to antecedently given meanings. Rather they determine the meanings of words. Grammar is autonomous. Conceptual clarification is not to be conducted by depth-analysis, for nothing is hidden. The 'logical geology' of the Tractatus is replaced by 'grammatical topography', that is, by the

---

6   Wittgenstein (2001), p. 2. Translated from the original Latin text given by Wittgenstein.
7   Ibid., p. 4.

painstaking description of the use of words, of their modes of con-
text-dependence, and of their roles in action and interaction.[8]

A fear in turning to the use of Wittgenstein would be a fear that any
philosophy which takes language as its centre would be automatically
exclusionary of a person without language. However what Wittgenstein
does in the *Philosophical Investigations* is to lift the burden of language
by refusing to over-weight it with meaning. And, of course, one does
not need to speak in order to be engaged in a language game. Adam
does not appreciate the social context of language games, but, not-
withstanding that, they are going on around him all the time. By his
silence he is playing a key part within them, greater often than those
who have 'speaking roles'.

This way of thinking of the *Philosophical Investigations* has interesting consequences for theology and for ecclesiology. These are clear
if we treat contemporary Anglicanism as an (admittedly very large)
language game. Wittgenstein alerts us to the need for attentive scrutiny – 'painstaking description' – of our language as such, in its immediacy – 'nothing is hidden'. We should not necessarily assume that
conceptual clarification will lead us anywhere, or that the ideas which
our language describes can themselves be described as 'true' or 'false'.
The church has rules by which language can be used – some of us
call this 'orthodoxy' – we cannot assume that the rules by which any
language is used are correct or incorrect. Language cannot be mapped
onto antecedent meaning – what we might call tradition. However,
one word stands out. While concepts may not be 'true' or 'false', they
can be 'useful' within the game, and in maintaining the game. As we
give attentive scrutiny to our language, this is the test which should
be applied to it.

If we were to leave things there, not enough would have been
said. The work of Wittgenstein marked the linguistic turn, the turn
towards language. We have already considered the different ways in
which language relates to objects in the world. Contemporary with
Wittgenstein was a rather different turn, a turn toward the objects

---

8   P.M.S. Hacker, 'Wittgenstein, Ludwig Josef Johann (1889–1951)', *Oxford Dictionary
of National Biography*, Oxford University Press, September 2004; online edn, October
2008 [http://www.oxforddnb.com/view/article/36986, accessed 20 November
2008, subscription necessary].

in themselves. The word *phenomenology* covers a wide range of philosophical beliefs. Dermot Moran in his textbook of the same title gives a suggestive summary of what phenomenology actually is:

> It claims first and foremost to be a *radical* way of doing philosophy, a *practice* rather than a system. Phenomenology is best understood as a radical, anti-traditional style of philosophy, which emphasizes the attempt to get to the truth of matters, to describe the *phenomena*, in the broadest sense as whatever appears in the manner which it appears, that is as it manifests itself to consciousness, to the experiencer. As such, phenomenology's first step is to seek to avoid all misconstructions and impositions placed upon experience in advance, whether these are drawn from religious or cultural traditions, from everyday common sense, or indeed from science itself. Explanations are not to be imposed before the phenomena have been understood from within.[9]

Simone de Beauvoir recalled a famous encounter between Raymond Aron and Jean-Paul Sartre, at the Bec de Gaz in the Rue Montparnasse:

> We ordered the speciality of the house, apricot cocktails; Aron said, pointing to his glass: 'You see, my dear fellow, if you were a phenomenologist, you could talk about this cocktail glass and make philosophy out of it.' Sartre turned pale with emotion at this. Here was just the thing he had been longing to achieve for years – to describe objects just as he saw and touched them, and extract philosophy from the process.

On his way home from this encounter, on the Boulevard Saint-Michel, Sartre purchased Levinas' book on Edmund Husserl, considered to be the founder of phenomenology, and 'leafed through the volume as he walked along, without even having cut the pages'.[10]

One particular feature of Husserl's thinking is 'bracketing', sometimes called epoché – abstaining from positing the existence of the world of experience. David Woodruff Smith in his *Husserl* described the sequence of thought which is entailed by bracketing.

1. My consciousness is usually a consciousness of something.

---

9   Moran (2000), p. 4.

10   De Beauvoir (1965), pp. 135–136.

Then comes the act of 'bracketing', which bears a similarity – but only a similarity – to the radical doubt of Descartes.

2. In order to shift my attention away from objects in the world around me, I bracket the thesis of the existence of the world including those objects.

3. I then attend to my consciousness of objects in the world.

4. In this modified attitude towards the world, I give phenomenological descriptions of various types of experience just as I experience them, where these descriptions characterize the contents or meanings of such experiences, presenting objects as experienced, regardless of whether the objects represented by those meanings exist.[11]

One of the major difficulties with the phenomenological reduction is whether it is actually possible to perform it. If the intention of phenomenology is to go to the objects themselves, without pre-interpretation, refusing to allow interpretation to stand in the way between us and the objects which surround us from day to day, it could be argued that interpretation will always hold its ground, will not allow itself to be dislodged. Merleau-Ponty says that 'all [phenomenology's] efforts are concentrated upon re-achieving a direct and primitive contact with the world, and endowing that contact with a philosophical status'.[12] It is an effort which creates difficulties. Much light is shed upon these difficulties if we seek to fit Adam within the schema proposed by Woodruff Smith. I suspect – but, of course, cannot prove – that (1) is not applicable to Adam, in the sense that it is unlikely that he will, following (2), have formed a 'thesis of the existence of the world'. I am here broadening the existing thinking about autism, as the effect of a deficit in 'theory of mind', to suggest that, at least in the case of some people with autism, they may well be living 'theory free'. Adam is thus free, following (3), to attend to his consciousness of objects in the world. This is certainly the experience of being with him on any given day: his attention is to the immediacy of objects, and to the stimulation that those objects, especially the objects of his

11   Woodruff Smith (2007), p. 242.
12   Merleau-Ponty (2002), p. vii.

obsessions, can give him. The thought is to some extent confirmed by Olga Bogdashina's account of sensory experiences in autism:

> Autistic people seem to perceive everything as it is. It is sort of 'literal perception', for example, they may *see* things without interpretation and understanding. Professor [Allan] Snyder, [Director of the Centre for the Mind, University of Sydney, Australia] who studies the phenomenon of autistic savants, suggests that autistic people look at the world the way it actually is.[13]

Bogdashina also cites the words of Jared Blackburn, who is a person with autism: 'Most things I would take at face value, without judging or interpreting them. I look at them in a concrete, literal, and very individual way.'[14] For Jean-Paul Sartre his experience with the apricot cocktail was a momentary revelation, which may be said to have become a way of life. For Adam, this immediacy of physical objects may well always have been his way of life. However, it is not likely that he then follows (4): he simply does not give descriptions (phenomenological or otherwise) of various types of experience, nor does he characterize the contents or meanings of such experiences. There are those who might argue that the phenomenological reduction is impossible. I would want to argue that while difficult, it is not impossible, and that it is enabled by engaging imaginatively with the world of Adam and those like him. To do that we have to theorize about Adam's mind – and it will be noted that I have been deliberately cautious in talking of likelihoods rather than certainties – in ways which he cannot do about the minds of those around him. This can be achieved by approaching Adam as he is, without pre-interpretation.

Thus, I would very much affirm the way of making a systematic theology which is identified with the names of Rudolf Bultmann and John Macquarrie, which draws upon the existentialist tradition which arose from the work of Husserl, and has its roots further back in Kierkegaard. One particular aspect of that tradition which I need to pick out is ethical, a situationalist ethics. Such an ethics is not necessarily affirmed by all existentialists, but is of a piece with the overall phenomenological stance of approaching existence without prior

---

13   Bogdashina (2003), p. 45.
14   Loc. cit.

interpretation. That stance is challenged whenever a Christian community forms an ethics to deal with a specific ethical problem, to make ethics applicable, and to lay down guidelines for future action. If the challenges which I faced in lived experience had been, for example, to do with human sexuality or stem-cell research there are abundant sources of ethical direction, and indeed a whole range of discordant voices, to any one of which I might have chosen to listen. However, the ethical challenge which I faced was how to respond to autism, how adequately to discharge my parental responsibilities, and how to gain access to public services. Aspects of my situation are considered within the canon of Christian ethical teaching: the Christian Church in any of its denominations would, for example, have something to say about responsible parenting. Yet Christian ethical teaching, like so much else in the world, offers a source of generic support, rather than being autism specific. The Church seeks to make its ethical teaching more specifically applicable through its systems of pastoral care, yet I have met many priests over the last ten years, including those in positions of seniority, who – I must stress, through no fault of their own – could not be said to be autism aware. In these circumstances, and bearing in mind the added weight which Adam's own way of being would give to this response, I was thrown back upon an existentialist, situationalist ethic. The moment when this was most true was on the day in which Adam went into full-time care. Even with a priest whose judgement I did – and do – trust standing alongside, there was no moral compass with which to get my bearings in an extreme situation, other than seeking, as I went along, to respond in a Christian and a human way to that situation. It was the situation itself which gave me my moral bearings. The criticism of a situationalist ethic is that there is no regulation over the outcome, that one who is engaged in a given situation can do exactly as they like. I would rather see it as being morally constrained by the situation, to an intense degree.

I now turn to examine those developments in subsequent, especially continental philosophy, and especially those philosophies which are characterized by Gary Gutting in his book *French Philosophy in the Twentieth Century* as 'philosophies of difference'. It will be grasped immediately that such a philosophy would be of interest having spent so much time in the company of one whose very life is 'difference'. 'The general theme of difference is,' Gutting tells us, 'fundamental for all poststructuralists, who are in principle wary of thought that reduces diverse elements to the sameness of unifying concepts or theories.'[15] From the different thinkers whom Gutting considers in his chapter on philosophies of difference, it is useful to pick out one, Gilles Deleuze, whose 'thought develops out of two "fundamental" intuitions, one of being, the other of the thinking whereby being is grasped. The first intuition is that being is radically diverse, the second that, correspondingly, thought is a recognition of ontological diversity, not a reduction to unity.' The first intuition recognizes Adam's full participation in the realm of being, which, as with other disabled people, is so much more conceded in theory than in fact. The second intuition recognizes as central to thought the way in which – we may presume – Adam thinks, by refusing to reduce things in thought to coherent unity. One may suspect that reality appears to Adam in glorious diversity, not pieced together.

From this comes the postmodern suspicion of metanarratives, those accounts of personal and collective history which attempt to impose coherence on the diversity of human experience both collective and personal. The Christian Church is the trustee of one such metanarrative, which is the Christian account of salvation. It is also the case that the Christian Church, especially within the Anglican tradition, treats diversity as a problem. As an Anglican priest, while wanting to maintain Christian orthodoxy, I could not, as a parent and carer, affirm those who treat diversity and difference as problematic. It may well be that we need to look at the next stage in the development of systematic theology, which examines the fruitful encounter between Christian systematics and philosophies of difference. It may well be that from postmodern philosophies of difference, Christian systematics needs to learn, not just how to handle, and manage difference – for that, again would be to treat it as a problem – but to transform our ways of seeing difference. I suspect that this work remains to be done.

The point of departure for the Algerian-French philosopher Jacques Derrida is the phenomenological tradition. His dissertation for the *diplôme d'études supérieures*, as well as his early published work,

---

15   Gutting (2001), p. 318. Chapter 11 covers philosophies of difference, pp. 318–352.

was on Husserl.[16] It is often commented, especially by his many critics, that Derrida's language is sometimes difficult to understand. I here reproduce a sample, taken almost at random from his work, to illustrate the point:

> So what are we to do? It is impossible to respond here. It is impossible to respond to this question about the response. It is impossible to respond to the question by which we precisely ask ourselves whether it is necessary to respond or not to respond, whether it is necessary, possible or impossible. The aporia without end paralyses us because it binds us doubly (I must and I need not, I must not, it is necessary and impossible, etc.). In one and the same place, on the same apparatus, I have my two hands tied or nailed down.[17]

This near incomprehensibility does not simply apply to Derrida's text: it was an especial characteristic of his verbal performance. Dermot Moran, writing before Derrida's death, described the public presentation of his ideas:

> Derrida is infamous for his highly stylized, self-reflexive, at times even self-indulgent, lecturing performances, during which he may speak without notes for many hours at a time, exhibiting a powerful memory, as he traces and retraces his own attempts and failures ('aporias', i.e. blockages, dead ends) to get to grips with a certain text or train of thought. One such talk given over two days and lasting six hours has been published as *Aporias*.[18]

Derrida's verbal capacity and Adam's non-verbal world would seem to be wholly opposite to each other, images of each other. They are in fact opposite in the sense that they are mirror images. The interest of Derrida is in fact in that for which he is most condemned: his nearly incomprehensible use of language. The interest lies in that he is taking language to its own borders, stretching meaningful language to its limits. The above quotation was taken almost at random from his writings, but I must confess that the basis for its selection was in what followed it in the text:

---

16   *Edmund Husserl's Origin of Geometry: an introduction*, 1962.
17   Wood (ed.) (1992), p. 19. The passage is taken from Derrida's own chapter in a 'Critical Reader' on his work which is entitled Passions: 'an oblique offering'.
18   Moran (2000), p. 436.

> But also how is it that it [the aporia] does not prevent us from speaking, from continuing to describe the situation, from trying to make ourselves understood? What is the nature of this language, since already it no longer belongs, no longer belongs simply either to the question or the response whose limits we have just verified and are continuing to verify.

For some, *aporia* is a concept. I do not say this in any sense to belittle him, but suspect that Adam is a living experience of *aporia* as he wrestles, struggles with language. Derrida had a verbal fluency which is not Adam's, but their problems are the same.

At the heart of Derrida's thinking is one famous – or infamous – word: deconstruction. There are many accounts of this in the secondary literature on Derrida. This is taken from Barbara Johnson's introduction to Derrida's *Dissemination*:

> Western thought, says Derrida, has always been structured in terms of dichotomies or polarities : good vs. evil; being vs. nothingness, presence vs. absence, truth vs. error, identity vs. difference, mind vs. matter, man vs. woman, soul vs. body, life vs. death, nature vs. culture, speech vs. writing. These polar opposites do not, however, stand as independent and equal entities. The second term in each pair is considered the negative, corrupt, undesirable version of the first, a fall away from it. Hence, absence is the lack of presence, evil is the fall from good, error is a distortion of truth etc. In other words, the two terms are not simply opposed in their meanings, but are arranged in a hierarchical order which gives the first term *priority*, in both the temporal and qualitative sense of the word. In general, what these hierarchical oppositions do is to privilege unity, identity, immediacy and temporal and spacial *presentness* over distance, difference, dissimulation, and deferment.[19]

In this book, we have been concerned with a number of binary oppositions which are not mentioned here: ability and disability, understanding and cognitive impairment, power and weakness, sacred and secular, in which the first term, historically and otherwise, has been given priority over the second. By making use of Derrida's thought of deconstruction, we see that these issues belong with each other. One specific consequence of this is that the way in which the Church

---

19   Derrida (1981), p. viii.

handles the distinction between the sacred and secular – and I am clearly suggesting that this should be by the route of deconstruction, acknowledging the existence of their binary opposition, but refusing in daily *praxis* to prioritize one over the other – has immediate impacts upon other aspects of 'fundamental' human experience. The Church has there the possibility of modelling what deconstruction is, but equally borrows its sense of what deconstruction is from the realm of the secular.

In the processes of deconstruction, the questioning of language lies at the centre of Derrida's philosophy, and in particular in his holding up to question of the tradition of logocentrism. According to Moran, this word for Derrida 'sums up the essence of philosophy in the west in a single word'.[20] We are already getting some indication of the depth and width of the problem of language, a depth and width which is created by the sense of all philosophy turning around the word and centred upon it. In more detail, logocentrism

> refers to the manner in which the traditional prioritization of reason in philosophy has led to everything deemed irrational to be swept aside, treated as marginal and insignificant. Derrida claims the Western philosophical tradition is obsessed with being understood as presence (ontotheology) and with the universal nature of logic and rationality (logocentrism). Logocentrism, for Derrida, is tied to the assumption of a fixed foundational principle, which can be uniquely named whether it be 'being' or 'God'. The Greek word *logos* can mean reason, account, word or justification, and Derrida is playing with all these significations. The term 'logocentrism' implies the assumption of the centrality of the *logos*, of rationality, of logic, of the spoken word. The whole history of Western philosophy since the ancient Greeks has been circumscribed in the 'epoch of the *logos*' [...] perhaps best exemplified in the Christian doctrine of creation.[21]

This is a long quotation, but it is given here in order to show the all encompassing nature of Derrida's agenda, if agenda it can properly be called. The ground of Derrida's critique is actually in the inadequacy of language. Language does not work, as it appears to do. In

---

20   Ibid., p. 448.
21   Idem.

day-to-day life, the adequacy of language is taken for granted, perhaps because, in general terms, we do not have anything else which does what language does. However, there is, at the heart of our use of language, a misunderstanding: 'Logocentrism, for Derrida, is based on a profound misunderstanding of the relation between signifier and signified, namely the belief that a sign adequately represents its signified meaning, that language is a transparent window on reality.'[22] Adam has a classic diagnosis of autism with learning disabilities. It is assumed, because of his autism, which makes him (almost) non-verbal, that he is not able to create, for himself, and for others, a 'transparent window on reality'. The speculation here is that none of us are able to do that, that our understanding of language as such is based upon a profound misunderstanding. We all have a problem with language, but we are unaware of it, or were, until Derrida provided us with a diagnosis. According to Derrida, suggests Moran, 'there can never be a total or complete meaning, except as an ideal or indeed a fiction'.[23] Before we rush to describe non-verbal people with autism like Adam as 'impaired', as 'having a deficit', or indeed being disabled, we need to reflect much more carefully on what it is that – in our minds – Adam does not have.

The radical contention of this chapter is that the philosophy of language should be recast in the light of linguistic disability; that philosophy, our use of reason, should be recast in the light of learning disability, at the limits of reason. In such a short space, one can only indicate what such a project would look like, only point towards it. Should such a recasting of philosophy take place the project would then be to recast systematic theology as a result of the emergence of such a philosophy. Such a project would go to the heart of theology, as systematic theology is dependent upon Scripture, the church's inheritance of language. In the next chapter, let us re-read that language.

---

22   Idem.
23   Ibid., p. 471.

CHAPTER 6

Scripture and Tradition

Once we have examined our personal situation, asked the question 'why' about our situation, asked 'who' we are within that situation, and seen the contribution which secular thought can make to what many would see as essentially spiritual questions, then we are ready to approach Scripture and tradition. Often Christians go straight to Scripture and tradition, without reflecting on what should condition our reading of them.

Within the Anglican tradition it is said that there is a three legged stool to sustain faith and practice. As the *Virginia Report – the Report of the Inter-Anglican Theological and Doctrinal Commission from the 1998 Lambeth Conference* puts it: 'Anglicans are held together by the characteristic way in which they use Scripture, tradition and reason in discerning afresh the mind of Christ for the Church in each generation.'[1] Sometimes a fourth leg is added, that of experience. Sometimes reason and experience are conflated, with reason being taken as reflection upon personal and ecclesiastical experience. This book is all about reflection upon experience, in the light of Christian tradition. In the previous chapter, we have seen how Adam sits in relation to reason. I now turn my attention to Scripture, in its setting within the Christian tradition.

The starting point is that Adam simply does not have access to Scripture and tradition. He cannot read Scripture, even in a simplified form. He cannot hear and understand Scripture being read. Scripture

---

1   3.5.

is made up of language, and Adam does not have access to language. In the same way, I cannot pass on to him tradition of any kind, let alone Christian tradition. He cannot pass on tradition to anybody else. As a consequence of his inability to give consent, it is against the law for him to marry or have sexual intercourse. He will not have descendants.

At my ordination as a priest, I gave my overall assent to the historical formularies of the Anglican Church, including the Thirty-Nine Articles of Religion. The sixth of these indicates the theological challenge presented by Adam's inability to access Holy Scripture. The Old and New Testaments are central to the mystery of salvation:

> *VI. Of the Sufficiency of the Holy Scriptures for salvation* Holy Scripture containeth all things necessary to salvation: so that whatsoever is not read therein, nor may be proved thereby, is not to be required of any man, that it should be believed as an article of the Faith, or be thought requisite or necessary to salvation. In the name of the Holy Scripture we do understand those Canonical Books of the Old and New Testament, of whose authority was never any doubt in the Church.

I can and do entirely affirm the belief set out in this article. As a consequence of this biblically based faith, whenever my parishioners face pain and difficulty, either small or great, I would – and do – advise them to turn to the Bible for consolation, direction and encouragement. This was well put many centuries ago by Aelred of Rivaulx; in the series of sermons *De Oneribus [On the Burdens]* he wrote:

> Brothers, however cast down we may be by harassment or heartache, the consolations of Scripture will lift us up again for all the things that were written in former days were written for our instruction so that we, through steadfastness and the encouragement the Scriptures give us, might have hope. [Romans 15:4] I tell you, brothers, no misfortune can touch us, no situation so galling or distressing can arise that does not, as soon as Holy Writ seizes hold of us, either fade into nothingness or become bearable.[2]

There is here a certain circularity. What validates Scripture is Scripture itself – the familiar quotation from Romans 15 – and the

---

2   Matarasso (1993), p, 193.

consequences of reading Scripture. Into this circle Adam is not able to break. However, this is only the beginning of the theological and pastoral difficulty. The situation which Adam created around him can be adequately described in the terms which Aelred uses – 'harassment', 'heartache', 'galling', 'distressing'. It was exactly at the moment when I most needed the consolations of Scripture, which I would naturally seek, both as a priest and indeed as a Christian, that the way into Scripture became blocked. I cannot take a solution to the difficulties from which the source of those difficulties is – because of who he is – excluded. I do not believe that there is any set of circumstances in which the distress which I have known because of Adam will 'fade into nothingness or become bearable'. Within the Evangelical tradition, theologies of the Word of God often make absolute demands upon us as Christians. Often we do not realize that our theological terminology – in this case, the very word 'Word' – automatically excludes people with disabilities and/or their carers and prevents them from finding there anything for their comfort.

This is not to say that the Bible has not functioned in a new and fresh way in my heart and soul in the period since Adam's diagnosis. We have already seen that I take those experiences to be a radical expression of nothingness and meaninglessness. Many other people apart from myself experience life in that way. We could go so far as to say all, if we were but willing to admit it. The New Testament, particularly within the Passion narratives, provides an extended and nuanced commentary upon that human experience, culminating in the cry of Jesus upon the Cross: 'My God, my God, why have you forsaken me'. In the accounts of his ministry, Jesus is portrayed as the supremely able person – able to heal, skilful in teaching. In Mark 7:37, the crowds are so impressed by Jesus' healing work that they acclaim him: 'He has done all things well'. Nothing is so absurd as that all that ability, all that capability should find defeat upon the cross.

Karl Barth posited a theology of the Word which divided the world into the sacred and the secular. The revelation of God's Word divided up the world of the meaningful from that of the meaningless by creating meaning. *Contra* Barth, I have come to believe that the wonder of the cross is that – at the moment of salvation – meaning and meaninglessness are fused, and that it is at that point that salvation is won. The Fathers of the Council of Chalcedon in 451 promulgated as we have already discussed[3] their belief in the two natures of the Christ. Jesus was truly and fully divine, and truly and fully human – like unto us in every way except that he did not sin. The human and divine natures are not fused in one nature as the monophysites would have had it, but united in one person. The meaningful of the divine nature, and the absurdity of human existence are left in their integrity. On the cross, both natures know death: the sacred and the secular are fused together, and at that very moment our salvation is won. I would want to describe the years following Adam's diagnosis both as an experience of utter meaninglessness and an experience of salvation. I believe that the cross of Christ, and behind that the Scriptures in which the story of the Cross is set – and without which neither we, nor the Fathers of Chalcedon, would have known that story – provides me with a means of doing that without compromising the integrity of either side of that experience.

Hector Avalos has described the range of responses within disability studies to biblical studies: redemptionist, rejectionist and historicist:

> A 'redemptionist' approach seeks to redeem the biblical text, despite any negative stance on disabilities, by recontextualizing it for modern application [...] An opposing approach may be described as 'rejectionist' because it would argue that the Bible has negative portrayals of disability that should be rejected in modern society. The aim of such an approach is not to recontextualize but to repudiate. [...] A third approach may be called 'historicist', because it undertakes historical examinations of disabilities in the Bible and its subsequent interpretation, sometimes in comparison with neighbouring ancient cultures, without any overt interest in the consequences of the conclusions for modern application.[4]

It should be said that, because of my training as a historian, my first instinct is 'historicist': to try to get behind the texts, and their interpre-

---

3   See p. 61 for the previous discussion of Chalcedon. I seek here to show how that discussion fits in with questions of the place of Scripture, and with a biblically based faith.

4   Introduction, Avalos *et al.* (eds.) (2007), pp. 4–5, discussing Avalos' own article 'Redemptionism, rejectionism, and historicism in biblical studies' published in *Perspectives in Religious Studies*, Spring 2007.

tation of themselves, and our pre-interpretation of them, to get at the historical reality of life for a disabled person in the broad span of the biblical era. The sacredness of Scripture should not make it immune to the tests that are imposed upon any other texts, including the texts around it in the context of the ancient world. One should not allow one's desire to make a text applicable to a contemporary situation to transform the text itself, and to transform what lies behind it, the context from which it arose. However, once that process of 'historicist' interpretation has been undertaken and completed, then – and only then – one can examine the question of applicability. I will leave to the conclusion of this discussion whether I myself take a 'redemptionist' or 'rejectionist' approach to Scripture. Paradoxically, it would be possible to take a 'rejectionist' view while maintaining the 'high' view of the authority of Scripture that I have already outlined: if Scripture did not matter, and matter profoundly, one would have a more immediate way out of the questions which are raised by the 'rejectionist' view. It should finally be noted in this context that all those whose life is characterized by 'difference', be it on grounds of gender, sexual orientation, or disability, have similar problems with Scripture: whether to recontextualize or reject. It would seem, following Avalos, that – at very least – recontextualization is called for.

Among those whose approach could be characterized as going further than calling for recontextualization is John Hull, Professor of Religious Education in the University of Birmingham. In his book *In The Beginning There Was Darkness* he writes of the ways in which becoming a disabled person transformed his approach to biblical studies:

> We read the Bible through the world in which we ourselves are embedded. When I was sighted, I read the Bible as a sighted person because I was embedded in the sighted world. It did not occur to me that I was sighted; I was just a normal person. Then I became blind. After the initial shock and the sense of alienation from my former life and world, once again I became a normal person. But the Bible seemed to have become abnormal. It came from a strange world – the world of sighted people, which was no longer mine.[5]

---

5   Hull (2001), p. 3.

Although I am not reckoned to be a disabled person, the experience of caring for Adam triggered off a similar sequence. I belonged to a world which was not aware of autism, and it did not occur to me that I belonged to that world. I have traced in Chapter 2 the sense of shock and alienation, and the recovery of whatever 'normality' may be. I would perhaps call it everyday ordinariness. I recognize exactly Professor Hull's sense of the Bible belonging to a strange world, no longer mine. It must be like that for many people outside Church communities, for whom the Bible belongs to 'a strange world, not yet, and sometimes not ever mine'. The key is to enter into conversation. As Professor Hull puts it: 'In these chapters I will enter into conversation with the Bible from my point of view as a blind person.'[6] In my turn, and following a similar model, in these chapters I will enter into conversation with the Bible from my point of view of the parent/carer of a person with autistic spectrum disorder and attention deficit hyperactivity disorder.

As I have indicated, I believe that the starting point for this is dispassionate historical analysis, insofar as dispassionate historical analysis is available to us. This immediately poses some classic questions of hermeneutics. If autism belongs to that category of things which belong to the twentieth-century world, then one conjecture would be that what we call autism would be unknown to the New Testament writers. How is it possible to bring to bear on a subject a text whose authors knew nothing of that subject? Carers of those with autism are used to receiving help from public services which are generic rather than autism specific. Is it possible that the Bible falls into this category, of being generally useful, but not autism specific, that a misfit is created between the text and its direct application? However, another possibility exists: that although autism was not named before 1943, it existed, and had existed for a considerable time. In 2000, Rab Houston, Professor of Early Modern History at the University of St. Andrew's, and Uta Frith, Professor of Cognitive Development at the University of London, produced a fascinating study of the case in eighteenth-century Scotland of Hugh Blair of Borgue: the successful attempt in 1748 to annul Hugh Blair's marriage on the grounds of (that very contemporary issue of) mental incapacity. In *Autism in History – the case of*

---

6   Idem.

Hugh Blair of Borgue, Houston and Frith show the ways in which Hugh Blair's recorded behaviours in the mid-eighteenth century correspond to Kanner's description of autism in the mid-twentieth century. He had, according to the court records:

> poor speech and even poorer communication. He did not take part in the social life of the family or community. Many of his activities were baffling to others. He performed repetitive tasks unsuitable for his station in life, such as carrying stones. He insisted on having the same place at church and, according to a former servant of the family, 'was very careful to set anything right that was in any way out of order in the house.[7]

He had a good memory and, by coincidence, shared with one of Kanner's subjects the ability to recite the Presbyterian catechism. This takes us back as far as the eighteenth century. There are those who argue, although autism did not 'exist' within medical discourse, was not named in an earlier period, that it presents itself in the form of folktale. As Francesca Happé tells us: 'Almost certainly, autism has always existed. Folktales can be found in almost every culture which tell stories of naïve or "simple" individuals with odd behaviour and a striking lack of common sense.' She herself supplies stories from India, from Malta, and from the Ashanti tribe.[8] If this is the case – and the case is difficult to prove, since people with autism, outside folktale, would leave little historical trace – then people with autism would have been known to the biblical writers. Their writings about people whom we would identify as having mental health problems or learning disabilities sit, as folktale, alongside other ancient stories about people with autism, and can be read in that context.

I am now going to turn to a series of specific biblical texts, whose re-reading and reinterpretation has proved fruitful for me in recent years. It will not be a surprise that I am going to turn first of all to the Book of Job. This book gives us a theological response to a situation of suffering, of the response of a person who is *in extremis*. Marilyn

---

7   Houston and Frith (2000), p. 97.
8   Happé (1994), pp. 7–8, 128–129.

McCord Adams uses the term 'horrendous evils'.[9] As I moved through my own extreme experience I had the sense of the accumulation of these things, which I hope I have been already been able to convey in these pages. The Book of Job captures very well that way of being, of one damned thing after another.

BOOK OF JOB 1:13–21

> Now there was a day when his sons and daughters were eating and drinking wine in their eldest brother's house; and there came a messenger to Job, and said, 'The oxen were ploughing and the asses feeding beside them; and the Sabeans fell upon them and took them, and slew the servants with the edge of the sword; and I alone have escaped to tell you.' While he was yet speaking, there came another, and said, 'The fire of God fell from heaven and burned up the sheep and the servants, and consumed them; and I alone have escaped to tell you.' While he was yet speaking, there came another, and said, 'The Chaldeans formed three companies, and made a raid upon the camels and took them, and slew the servants with the edge of the sword; and I alone have escaped to tell you.' While he was yet speaking, there came another, and said, 'Your sons and daughters were eating and drinking wine in their eldest brother's house; and behold, a great wind came across the wilderness, and struck the four corners of the house, and it fell upon the young people, and they are dead; and I alone have escaped to tell you.' Then Job arose, and rent his robe, and shaved his head, and fell upon the ground, and worshipped. And he said, 'Naked I came from my mother's womb, and naked shall I return; the Lord gave, and the Lord has taken away; blessed be the name of the Lord.'

JOB 2:7–13

> So Satan went forth from the presence of the Lord, and afflicted Job with loathsome sores from the sole of his foot to the crown of his head. And he took a potsherd with which to scrape himself, and sat among the ashes. Then his wife said to him, 'Do you still hold

---

9   In the title of her 1999 work *Horrendous Evils and the Goodness of God* (Cornell University Press), as well as in her contribution to the Oxford University Press collection *The Problem of Evil*, which she also co-edited, in 1990.

fast your integrity? Curse God, and die.' But he said to her, 'You speak as one of the foolish women would speak. Shall we receive good at the hand of God, and shall we not receive evil?' In all this Job did not sin with his lips. Now when Job's three friends heard of all this evil that had come upon him, they came each from his own place, Eliphaz the Temanite, Bildad the Shuhite, and Zophar the Naamathite. They made an appointment together to come to condole with him and comfort him. And when they saw him from afar, they did not recognize him; and they raised their voices and wept; and they rent their robes and sprinkled dust upon their heads toward heaven. And they sat with him on the ground seven days and seven nights, and no-one spoke a word to him, for they saw that his suffering was very great.

The author of the Book of Job makes an early entry into the age-old question as to why bad things happen: according to Gutiérrez, writing in 1986, 'there is agreement today that it was written between 500 and 350 BC, probably in the province of Judea'.[10] In the passage before these he portrays a deal between God and Satan, in which God permits Satan to put Job to the test. God places in Satan's hand all that Job has. Thus the narrative avoids putting ultimate responsibility upon God. However, in this first passage, the author of Job suggests a further threefold classification. The destruction originates from 'the fire of God' – possibly lightning – from disturbance in the realm of human sociability – the aggression of the Chaldean companies, and from disturbance within the realm of the natural world – the great wind across the wilderness. Following a further audience between God and Satan, Job suffers a further affliction, that of illness, 'loathsome sores from the sole of his foot to the crown of his head'. In short, the trouble comes from God, humanity, and nature. Nature is bifurcated into the external natural world and the internal suffering of the body in its totality. Job's response is a turn towards the unadorned self, and that self turned towards worship: he 'rent his robe, and shaved his head, and fell upon the ground, and worshipped'. In the next chapter, we shall look at what it is to worship from within a situation of extremity. Job here in turn is surrounded by elective silence. When his three 'comforters' arrive they sit with him without speech, in silence for seven days.

---

10   Gutiérrez (1987), p. 107.

JOB 40:1–7

And the Lord said to Job: 'Shall a faultfinder contend with the Almighty? He who argues with God, let him answer it.' Then Job answered the Lord: 'Behold, I am of small account; what shall I answer thee? I lay my hand on my mouth. I have spoken once, and I will not answer; twice, but I will proceed no further.' Then the Lord answered Job out of the whirlwind: 'Gird up your loins like a man; I will question you, and you declare to me.'

At the end of the book, Job expresses his submission to God in two speeches of which this is the first. As the beginning of the extended discourse with God and his friends, so now Job elects for silence, this time with God rather than with his friends. What I am suggesting is that Adam in his non-elective silence is very close to the most fundamental, the most primordial response to the challenges which the created world offers to us.

JOB 42:1–6

Then Job answered the Lord: 'I know that thou canst do all things, and that no purpose of thine can be thwarted. "Who is this that hides counsel without knowledge?" Therefore I have uttered what I did not understand, things too wonderful for me, which I did not know. "Hear, and I will speak; I will question you, and you declare to me." I had heard of thee by the hearing of the ear, but now my eye sees thee; therefore I despise myself, and repent in dust and ashes.'

This is the second of Job's submissions to God. It is separated from the first by a chapter which is at least in part a celebration of divine capacity relative to human incapacity. The first two verses of that chapter set the tone: 'Can you draw out Leviathan with a fishhook, or press down his tongue with a cord? Can you put a rope in his nose, or pierce his jaw with a hook?' It is to this that Job now responds, acknowledging that divine capacity: 'I know that thou canst do all things...' Capacity and disability are in some way objective; in another way they are socially constructed by the interpretation which is placed upon them. In the narrative of the Book of Job, God gives a statement of His objective power; Job in his response provides the interpretation of divine capacity and his own disability. He expresses his relative disability in terms of cognitive impairment: 'I have uttered what I did not understand…' Job is thus reduced to elective silence, while God insists upon verbal relationship: 'Hear, and I will speak; I will question you, and you declare to me.' This brings us to a wider problem in the salvation history of the Old and New Testaments. The God of the Scriptures in the face of his recalcitrant people is constantly insisting upon engagement, conversation, and socialization: as we have seen[11] this takes place from the moment of creation; it continues in the processes of recreation, of salvation.

From this Old Testament text, we turn to the New Testament, which is unusual as an historic document and as a document of its own period in giving a prominence within its narrative to the physically ill, the disabled, the disturbed, the excluded. Without them, the New Testament documents, and certainly the Gospels would be very different texts indeed.

LUKE 2:40–52 (ONLY IN LUKE)

And the child grew and became strong, filled with wisdom; and the favour of God was upon him. Now his parents went to Jerusalem every year at the feast of the Passover. And when he was twelve years old, they went up according to custom; and when the feast was ended, as they were returning, the boy Jesus stayed behind in Jerusalem. His parents did not know it, but supposing him to be in the company they went a day's journey, and they sought him among their kinsfolk and acquaintances; and when they did not find him, they returned to Jerusalem, seeking him. After three days they found him in the temple, sitting among the teachers, listening to them and asking them questions; and all who heard him were amazed at his understanding and his answers. And when they saw him they were astonished; and his mother said to him, 'Son, why have you treated us so? Behold, your father and I have been looking for you anxiously.' And he said to them, 'How is it that you sought me? Did you not know that I must be in my Father's house?' And they did not understand the saying which he spoke to them. And he went down with them and came to Nazareth, and

---

11   See p. 80.

was obedient to them; and his mother kept all these things in her heart. And Jesus increased in wisdom and in stature, and in favour with God and man.

The first verse given here is the last verse of the preceding passage, which is the account, also only in Luke, of Jesus' parents taking him as a baby to the Jewish Temple for the rite of purification, and there meeting with Simeon and Anna. However, it is given here, as it also frames this passage in its parallel with verse 52. 'And the child grew and became strong, filled with wisdom; and the favour of God was upon him' becomes 'and Jesus increased in wisdom and in stature, and in favour with God and man'. We will later in this chapter examine passages in which Jesus becomes the excluded other. As a baby he has the favour of God; as he moves beyond his twelfth year, he is 'in favour with God and man'. He is finding acceptance in human society. We have already considered the possibilities of the interpretation of autism using the phenomenological tradition. Merleau-Ponty, a key figure within that tradition, in his account of the self and others, embeds reference to that great name in child development, Piaget:

> At about twelve years old, says Piaget, the child achieves the *cogito*,[12] and reaches the truths of rationalism. At this stage, it is held, he discovers himself both as a point of view on the world, and also as called upon to transcend that point of view, and to construct an objectivity at the level of judgment. Piaget brings the child to a mature outlook as if the thoughts of the adult were self-sufficient and disposed of all contradictions. But, in reality, it must be the case that the child's outlook is in some vindicated against the adult's and against Piaget's, and that the unsophisticated thinking of our earliest years remains as an indispensable acquisition underlying that of maturity.[13]

We will look first at Piaget's thinking, and then turn to Merleau-Ponty's interpretation of him. Lukes elaborates here, over and above the material about Jesus' infancy contained in Matthew's Gospel, a particular aspect of the doctrine of the Incarnation. In the Incarnation, God experiences human experience, including the experience of mat-

---

12 See p. 78.
13 Merleau-Ponty (2002), pp. 413– 414. Merleau-Ponty is discussing Piaget's work of 1926, *La représentation du monde chez l'infant.*

uration, that experience of child development which Piaget among recent thinkers so much made his own. This is both cognitive and physical development: Jesus is said to increase in wisdom and in stature. If Piaget's description is right – and its rightness or otherwise is not really in question here – then we have in Luke a description of Jesus just as in a process of 'normal' development he emerges into the stage of rational thought, the point of positing his own identity as a reasoning being, and – having posited that identity – becoming capable of transcending his specific point of view. This last element is why it is so important that we have Him in the Temple, listening to them and asking *them* questions, and they, in turn, amazed at his understanding and answers. In one way, Luke is describing what he would imagine to happen if the Messiah came, as a young boy, to the Temple. In another way, he is describing a 'normal' process in which those who are taught replace in authority those who have taught. It is paralleled by the tense, adolescent exchanges between Jesus and his parents, by which he establishes his *de facto* independence from them, again in a dual role as Son of God, and simply as 'son'. This adolescent emergence is – crucially – expressed in reciprocal speech, especially in Jesus' relations with the Jewish teachers. The overall difficulty of this passage is that Luke's view of the Incarnation commits him not just to saying that God participated in processes of human development, but also to saying, problematically, that, because God is God, he could only have had a praiseworthily 'normal' human development. When Luke says that Jesus increased in wisdom and in stature, he is recording the belief that Jesus was not a person with disabilities. Piaget, in Merleau-Ponty's account, is shown to believe that the stages of development are successive: first there is childhood, and then, at about the age of 12, the emergence of rationality and of the rational cogito. *Contra* Piaget, Merleau-Ponty suggests that the thinking of childhood is vindicated against the adult, that 'the unsophisticated thinking of our earliest years remains as an indispensable acquisition underlying that of maturity'. There is an element of childhood's vindication of itself in the scene with the teachers in the Temple. Following Merleau-Ponty, what I am suggesting is that the pre-rational remains with us as we change and develop. What Adam is – indefinitely pre-rational, without the foreclosure of rationality upon the prerational world – is indefinitely with us. In the most straightforward of terms, this would account for the social priority which Jesus is later to give to the very smallest of children.

MARK 1:23–26 (WITH PARALLEL IN LUKE 4:33–35)

> And immediately there was in their synagogue a man with an unclean spirit; and he cried out, 'What have you to do with us, Jesus of Nazareth? Have you come to destroy us? I know who you are, the Holy One of God.' But Jesus rebuked him, saying, 'Be silent, and come out of him!' And the unclean spirit, convulsing him and crying with a loud voice, came out of him.

This passage marks the introduction within St. Mark's Gospel of the key theme of the Messaianic Secret: Jesus' refusal to disclose his own identity or to allow others to do so. It is ironic that much of the early development in Christian history centred on questions of Christology, around determining the identity of the Christ within the scheme of salvation. Christ himself, at least in St. Mark's Gospel, is discreet on this point. The writer of the Gospel, like any good narrator, allows himself to be 'in on the secret', that is of the true identity of Jesus. It is so immediately part of the Gospel texts that they make a claim to be dealing with salvation itself that we are often in some way unconscious of that claim. St. Mark puts at centre stage in the drama of salvation that which is unsaid, that which does not belong to discourse. St. Mark's Christ exists in solidarity with those whose identity is difficult to perceive. So often, in the case of specific disabilities, there are calls for an 'awareness raising campaign'. That is exactly because the identities of individuals with disabilities are difficult to perceive, difficult to interpret.

MARK 5:1–20 (WITH PARALLELS IN MATTHEW 8:28–34 AND LUKE 8:26–39)

> They came to the other side of the sea, to the country of the Gerasenes. And when he had come out of the boat, there met him out of the tombs a man with an unclean spirit, who lived among the tombs; and no-one could bind him anymore, even with a chain;

for he had often been bound with fetters and chains, but the chains he wrenched apart, and the fetters he broke in pieces; and no-one had the strength to subdue him. Night and day among the tombs and on the mountains he was always crying out, and bruising himself with stones. And when he saw Jesus from afar, he ran and worshipped him; and crying out with a loud voice, he said, 'What have you to do with me, Jesus, Son of the Most High God? I adjure you by God, do not torment me.' For he had said to him, 'Come out of the man, you unclean spirit!' And Jesus asked him, 'What is your name?' He replied, 'My name is Legion; for we are many.' And he begged him eagerly not to send them out of the country. Now a great herd of swine was feeding there on the hillside; and they begged him, 'Send us to the swine, let us enter them.' So he gave them leave. And the unclean spirits came out, and entered the swine; and the herd, numbering about two thousand, rushed down the steep bank into the sea, and were drowned in the sea. The herdsmen fled, and told it in the city and in the country. And people came to see what it was that had happened. And they came to Jesus, and saw the demoniac sitting there, clothed and in his right mind, the man who had had the legion; and they were afraid. And those who had seen it told what had happened to the demoniac and to the swine. And they began to beg Jesus to depart from their neighbourhood. And as he was getting into the boat, the man who had been possessed with demons begged him that he might be with him. But he refused, and said to him, 'Go home to your friends, and tell them how much the Lord has done for you, and how he has had mercy on you.' And he went away and began to proclaim in the Decapolis how much Jesus had done for him; and all men marvelled.

This passage sits within St. Mark's Gospel as a doublet with the healing of the daughter of Jairus, the ruler of the synagogue: the distinction is made between the mental and physical illness. Before any other information is offered, the writer of the Gospel provides his readers with a diagnosis: here is a man 'with an unclean spirit'. As in any historical period, there is an attempt to interpret those with mental health problems, or those who are not what is called neurotypical. In a contemporary setting, we would ask what has 'caused' a particular set of presenting 'symptoms'. In this particular culture, explanatory force is given to the idea that the man 'has an unclean spirit'. The difficulty is that the biblical interpretation, in part because of the cultural authority of Scripture, has cast a very long shadow. In 1900, Cosmo Gordon Lang published a collection of essays *The Miracles of Jesus as Marks of the Way of Life*. A year later he was Bishop of Stepney, eight years later Archbishop of York, and 28 years later Archbishop of Canterbury. The first section of his chapter on the Gadarene Demoniac is headed 'disordered life'.[14] In keeping with his liberal Catholic belief, he skirts the question of what actually happened: 'Our business is not to explain the miracles, but to try to learn the lessons of life of which they were the signs.' He acknowledges that Jesus was accepting of the belief systems which he found around him, but with the implication that he probably knew better: 'How far Jesus in this, as manifestly he did in other matters, accommodated himself to the belief of the time, or to the illusions of the maniacs themselves – dealt with them on their own level for their lasting good we cannot tell.'[15] Then we come to the chief problem in all of this: 'But it is hardly possible to doubt that the authority of Jesus is given to the belief that these cases of mania were due, not only to disordered tissues of the brain, but to some mysterious possession of evil spirits.'[16] Lang has to some extent accomplished what would be called in a later generation the demythologization of the biblical account, but what has not gone away is what can only be described as biblically-inspired condescension to those whose challenges to wider society belong to the brain rather than the body: 'For our part we must be content to take this Gadarene demoniac simply as a type of human life when it has lost its self control and wanders disordered and confused, the mere prey of morbid passion or delusion.'[17] Lang's book on the miracles has a certain historical curiosity. I have included his comments here simply in order to contrast them with a much more recent exegesis of the same passage. To a recent collection of articles published by the Society of Biblical Literature, Holly Joan Toensing, who wrote with direct personal experience of mental illness,[18] contributed "'Living among the tombs" – society, mental

---

14   Lang (1900), p. 187ff.
15   Ibid., p. 188.
16   Ibid., p. 188.
17   Ibid., p. 188.
18   Her brother had likely, though undiagnosed, paranoid schizophrenia. Avalos *et al.* (eds.) (2007), p. 131ff.

illness and self-destruction in Mark 5:1–20'. In her article, she speaks
of the negative effect which the authority of Scripture, and indeed of
Jesus himself, have had on the lives of those with mental illness: 'Given
the fact that throughout most of Western history people believed that
behaviours associated with what we call mental illness today were
caused literally by demon possession, the demoniac story of Mark 5
and others like it certainly contributed to the stigmatization and ill
treatment of the mentally ill.' She continues with a description of the
strong version of the argument, of which Lang's exegesis is the weaker
and 'demythologized' form: 'Mentally ill persons were perceived as
weak willed or flawed in some way to have given the demon – even
Satan himself – a foothold in their lives , even welcoming it.'[19]

As interpreters of Scripture we need to be acutely and sensitively
aware of the implications of all this, not just for those with mental
health problems, but for those with severe learning disabilities and
associated challenging behaviours. The whole question needs to be
set in its cultural context, but in a very different way to the attempt
which Lang made to do this: in first-century Palestinian society, as in
others, a person with a disability or a mental health problem is treated
as unclean, is relegated to the margins. We would call it discrimination. The point is that Jesus breaks the purity taboo by associating
with those who have been marginalized. The marginalization is so
complete that the man lives 'among the tombs', on the margins of
life itself. He has been the victim of the classic response of society to
those with severe challenging behaviours or mental health problems,
the impulse towards control: he has been bound with chains, which
he has broken. Once those bonds have been broken, his true self is revealed in an uncontrolled state. His difficulties are with expressive language and with self-harming behaviour. Elsewhere within this book,
I will discuss the complex issues arising from the place of those with
learning disabilities within Christian and other religious worship. It
is striking that on his first encounter with Jesus, this man's response
is to offer him worship. We have already seen that Jesus as the Christ
challenges the assumptions of his own society by engaging with those
on the margins. The man seeks to further explore the nature of that
engagement: 'what have you to do with me?' In Mark's Gospel, much

---

19   Ibid. p. 133.

is made of the Messianic secret: Jesus' unwillingness to reveal his own identity, and his disciples' misunderstanding of that identity. The man correctly reveals that identity in its highest form – 'son of the most high God' – echoing the awareness with which St. Mark begins his narrative: 'The beginning of the good news of Jesus Christ, the Son of God.'[20] This Christological cognition is the basis of the worship that the man offers to Jesus. What follows is a classic encounter between a therapist/healer on the one hand, and the one who is the target of that healing on the other. The therapist is taken to be the one with the centred, clearly delineated identity on the one hand, while on the other is the multiple or disrupted personality of the one who is to be healed of all of that. The contrast is between an identity which hovers between multiplicity and single identity – '*my* name is legion, *we* are many' and the single identity of 'Jesus, Son of the most high God'. Like many with disabilities, the man reacts adversely to the prospect of being healed: once 'healed', he will cease to be himself. He tells Jesus not to torment him exactly because Jesus has said to him: 'Come out of the man, you unclean spirit.' The healing itself, with its strange details about the drowning of a whole herd of swine, locates the story within the whole debate in the New Testament about the relationship of the Christ to the Jewish law.[21] The presence of the swine within an agricultural setting is taken as an indication that Jesus here has entered a gentile community, in which pigs could be used for food. It allows us to correlate the whole discussion of what is unclean according to the Jewish law, with the discussion of the ways in which those with disabilities are the 'excluded other'. Once the healing has taken place, the local populace has exactly the same problem as the man himself with the healing. The question which he asked himself was: 'Will I be the same once I have been healed?'; the question which the crowd asks is 'Is he the same person, now that he has been healed?' As Mark comments, 'they came to Jesus, and saw the demoniac sitting there, clothed and in his right mind, the man who had had the legion; and they were afraid'. Just as he had feared being healed, now they fear him, once healed. Jesus himself thus becomes the target of the exclusion which he might have been thought to have overcome: they beg

---

20 Mark 1:1.
21 See Chapter 8, p. 179.

him to leave the vicinity. Contrariwise, the man's state of inclusion is participation in coherent speech, his rediscovery of a peer group – his 'friends', his free movement within rural and urban settings, and his concomitant participation in the spreading of the Gospel. He wishes to follow Jesus, to remain as he is, to share the exclusion which Jesus is now undergoing, but is prevented from doing so.

LUKE 10:25–37 (ONLY IN LUKE)

> And behold, a lawyer stood up to put him to the test, saying, 'Teacher, what shall I do to inherit eternal life?' He said to him, 'What is written in the law? How do you read?' And he answered, 'You shall love the Lord your God with all your heart, and with all your soul, and with all your strength, and with all your mind; and your neighbour as yourself.' And he said to him, 'You have answered right; do this, and you will live.' But he, desiring to justify himself, said to Jesus, 'And who is my neighbour?' Jesus replied, 'A man was going down from Jerusalem to Jericho, and he fell among robbers, who stripped him and beat him, and departed, leaving him half dead. Now by chance a priest was going down that road; and when he saw him he passed by on the other side. So likewise a Levite, when he came to the place and saw him, passed by on the other side. But a Samaritan, as he journeyed, came to where he was; and when he saw him, he had compassion, and went to him and bound up his wounds, pouring on oil and wine; then he set him on his own beast and brought him to an inn, and took care of him. And the next day he took out two denarii and gave them to the innkeeper, saying, "Take care of him; and whatever more you spend, I will repay you when I come back." Which of these three, do you think, proved neighbour to the man who fell among the robbers?' He said, 'The one who showed mercy on him.' And Jesus said to him, 'Go and do likewise.'

What enters into play in this passage is the question of salvation itself. If one believes that there is such a thing as eternal life, there is no question conceivably more important than that which the lawyer frames, with the irony of a trick question. The consequence is that in this passage we encounter the fundamentals of Christianity, those things than which nothing more important can be thought. At the very moment when Luke's Gospel comes to this point, an important cross-cultural transition takes place: the heart of the Christian tradition does not belong to Christianity but to Judaism. The twin commandments describe two different kinds of reciprocity: the equidistance of loving one's neighbour as oneself; the non-equidistant relationship envisaged in the commandment to love God with all of one's heart, soul, strength and mind. In contrast to certain theologies of grace, the starting point of that non-equidistant relationship is humanity rather than the godhead. One calls to mind Auden's words: 'Let the more loving one be me…' Famously, the lawyer focuses upon the relationship with neighbour rather than with God. The task of lawyers at all times and in all places has been to regulate the relationship of any given individual with those around her/him. This is what lawyers do; it is a natural question for a lawyer. Those with caring responsibilities, for whom some of their key relationships have become problematic, know the ways in which those relationships get caught up within legal frameworks. Jesus' response to the lawyer shows that there is, in the processes of care, something beyond the legal frameworks. We shall examine the story of the Good Samaritan as a paradigmatic account of a single act of care. Need is of its nature penultimate. Like Job the man travelling from Jerusalem to Jericho is in need because he is still alive, although 'half dead'. In this case, the official, the expected sources of the help – the priest and the Levite – turn out to be wilfully ineffective. They do not get as far even as making an assessment of need but, seeing a potentially dangerous overall situation, 'pass by on the other side'. The man is thrown back upon informal, and because informal, unexpected sources of care. As is well known, there was considerable tension between the Jews and the Samaritans: Jesus is being heavily ironic in his dealings with the Jewish lawyer in suggesting that if he wishes to be saved he should fulfil the obligation of the law in the same way as a Samaritan.[22] As one who extends care, the Samaritan takes as his starting point the place in which the person in need finds himself. His compassion is not generalized: it arises from the actual sight of the man. His compassion addresses both the need – he pours oil and wine on the man's wounds – and the circumstances from which the need has arisen – he ensures that the man is taken to a safe shelter,

---

22   Cf. John 4:9: 'The Samaritan woman said to him, "How is it that you, a Jew, ask a drink of me, a woman of Samaria?" For Jews have no dealings with Samaritans.'

to the inn. His care is not a single event: it is continuous, once they both arrive at the inn. Crucially, when a cash transaction is necessary in order to secure that the care should continue, it is made without a budget: 'Take care of him; and whatever more you spend, I will repay you when I come back.' It is thus patterned upon our human relationship with God, which – as Jesus' dialogue with the lawyer has already suggested – should not be limited or curtailed. This passage starts with a verbalization of that which is central to Christian belief. The question of the status of words in themselves is echoed throughout this book. What happens in the course of this passage is that Jesus turns attention from the question of words to the question of *praxis*. However many theology books may be written on the technical questions of soteriology, the praxis of the good Samaritan remains lies at the heart of the mystery of salvation. Other things are of value, but not essential. Care offered and practised across the boundaries of difference is what gets us there. That is what salvation is.

MARK 10:46–52 (WITH PARALLELS IN MATTHEW 20:29–34 AND LUKE 18:35–43)

> And they came to Jericho; and as he was leaving Jericho with his disciples and a great multitude, Bartimaeus, a blind beggar, the son of Timaeus, was sitting by the roadside. And when he heard that it was Jesus of Nazareth, he began to cry out and say, 'Jesus, Son of David, have mercy on me!' And many rebuked him, telling him to be silent; but he cried out all the more, 'Son of David, have mercy on me!' And Jesus stopped and said, 'Call him.' And they called the blind man, saying to him, 'Take heart; rise, he is calling you.' And throwing off his mantle he sprang up and came to Jesus. And Jesus said to him, 'What do you want me to do for you?' And the blind man said to him, 'Master, let me receive my sight.' And Jesus said to him, 'Go your way; your faith has made you well.' And immediately he received his sight and followed him on the way.

We have seen how earlier on in the Gospel account, one of the difficulties of reading is that Jesus imposes a cure upon disabled people. The parallels in Luke and Matthew are curious: Matthew has two blind men; in Luke, there is only one blind man. Only in Mark is this blind man identified as Bartimaeus, son of Timaeus. Mark in that way, over and above the other Gospels, identifies a disabled person as an individual, with his own, specific family context, rather than allowing the disability to be the identifier. There is a contrast with the earlier story of Legion, where the man's self-given name is definitive of his disability. Moreover, Jesus is not here imposing a cure. His question to Bartimaeus is significant: 'What do you want me to do for you?' It is especially significant within the narrative that this occurs as the last of Jesus miracles apart from his rather irate cursing of the fig tree.[23] What I am suggesting is a view of the Gospel which will allow for change and development in the person and ministry of Jesus. As ever, there is a danger of allowing our sense of Christ's divinity to prevent us from grasping his humanity. If human, He is, because human, constantly changing and developing. Failing to be aware of individual humanity is not just something which happens to those with disability. What I am further suggesting is that there is portrayed here, at what is in the Gospel narrative a moment of crisis, a turning point, a radical change in Jesus' attitude to disability, where the starting point is not the healer, but the person with disabilities her/himself, even though, as John Hull points out, as he reflects upon his own answer to Jesus' question, the response of Bartimaeus, as a disabled person, is conditioned by the values of the non-disabled world: 'To be delivered from the restrictions of blindness into the freedom of a sighted person's life is one of the most desirable persons that a sighted person could imagine. Naturally, blind people get caught up in this point of view.'[24] Everything at this point is tied up with the question of power, the power relations of the able and the disabled. In the previous pericope, James and John have made a bid for power in the Kingdom of God, exciting the annoyance of the other ten disciples. They do not want to be like Bartimaeus, disabled and consequently impoverished. They want thrones rather than the edge of the road: 'And James and John, the sons of Zebedee, came forward to him, and said to him, "Teacher, we want you to do for us whatever we ask of you." And he said to them, "What do you want me to do for you?" And they said to him, "Grant us to sit, one at your right hand and one at your left, in your

---

23 Mark 11:12–14, 19–22, with parallel in Matthew.
24 Hull (2001), p. 45.

glory.'"[25] The question which Jesus poses to James and John is exactly the same as the one which he will shortly pose to Bartimaeus: 'What do you want me to do for you?' In a Gospel which returns again and again to the theme of the disciples' misunderstanding of Jesus' message, we are not surprised that Jesus points out their mistake, locating himself differently within the operations of power, and locating his own Messianic calling within that relocation. 'But it shall not be so among you; but whoever would be great among you must be your servant, and whoever would be first among you must be slave of all. For the Son of man also came not to be served but to serve, and to give his life as a ransom for many.'[26] It is with heavy irony that Mark then has Bartimaeus address Jesus as 'Master'.

MARK 11:1–11

> And when they drew near to Jerusalem, to Bethphage and Bethany, at the Mount of Olives, he sent two of his disciples, and said to them, 'Go into the village opposite you, and immediately as you enter it you will find a colt tied, on which no-one has ever sat; untie it and bring it. If any one says to you, "Why are you doing this?" say, "The Lord has need of it and will send it back here immediately."' And they went away, and found a colt tied at the door out in the open street; and they untied it. And those who stood there said to them, 'What are you doing, untying the colt?' And they told them what Jesus had said; and they let them go. And they brought the colt to Jesus, and threw their garments on it; and he sat upon it. And many spread their garments on the road, and others spread leafy branches which they had cut from the fields. And those who went before and those who followed cried out, 'Hosanna! Blessed is he who comes in the name of the Lord! Blessed is the kingdom of our father David that is coming! Hosanna in the highest!' And he entered Jerusalem, and went into the temple; and when he had looked round at everything, as it was already late, he went out to Bethany with the twelve.

The beginning of the account of Christ's triumphant Messianic entry into Jerusalem is in Mark's Gospel a continuation of the Bartimaeus

---

25   Mark 10: 35–37.

26   Mark 10: 43–45.

story. That story began 'as he was leaving Jericho', and now Jesus is 'drawing near to Jerusalem'. The suspicion is at least partly confirmed by the conclusion of the account of the entry to Jerusalem, when Jesus goes into the Temple, and looks round at everything. He is using for himself the ability to see which he has given to Bartimaeus. The two accounts thus have, in Mark, a narrative integrity, which means that we can place the account of the taking of the colt within the context of the Bartimaeus story. 'The Lord has need of it' is a depiction of urgent need being met immediately, and upon request. One may surmise that although this is not salvation in itself, such a meeting of need is to be taken as the indication that the story is moving, both physically and in narrative terms, towards the salvific event. There are those – particularly those engaged in Christian social action – who might argue that the unconditional meeting of human need is salvation as such. The indication here is that it is a precondition, or at least a precursor of salvation.

MARK 14:63–65 (WITH PARALLELS IN MATTHEW 26:65–68 AND LUKE 22:71, AND 63–65)

And the high priest stood up in the midst, and asked Jesus, 'Have you no answer to make? What is it that these men testify against you?' But he was silent and made no answer. Again the high priest asked him, 'Are you the Christ, the Son of the Blessed?' And Jesus said, 'I am; and you will see the Son of man seated at the right hand of Power, and coming with the clouds of heaven.'

And the high priest tore his garments, and said, 'Why do we still need witnesses? You have heard his blasphemy. What is your decision?' And they all condemned him as deserving death. And some began to spit on him, and to cover his face, and to strike him, saying to him, 'Prophesy!' And the guards received him with blows.

We can see this scene at least in part in parallel with the story of Legion. In that story, Jesus enjoins silence regarding his own identity, and nonetheless Legion speaks. Here, Jesus is enjoined to speak, refuses speech, and then speaks to identify himself. In so doing he transcends or at least transgresses the boundary between silence and speech. We then move from the question of speech to the question of sight. Witnesses are definitionally those who have seen, or perceived that to which they bear witness. Jesus is then blindfolded. It is curious that the two Gospels which record this are Luke and Mark. Matthew's Gospel has a long diatribe against the Pharisees, which, as John Hull points out, uses language in which blindness becomes a term of abuse, part of an age-old tradition in which disability is used to denigrate, a tradition which persists to this day: 'Woe to you, blind guides' (23:16); 'You blind fools!' (23:17); 'You blind men!' (23:19); 'You blind guides' (23:24); 'You blind Pharisee!' (23:26).[27] This entire section of the diatribe and most of the rest disappears from Mark: what remains is directed at the scribes. Much of the passage disappears from Luke. Where there is a direct parallel, Luke replaces 'you blind Pharisee' with 'you fools', which, for those with learning disabilities, is scarcely an improvement. In the New Testament, taken as a whole, we get a sense of attitudes to disabled people that are not dissimilar to those of today: there is hostility, and there is an incoherent, inchoate response. However, at this point in the passion narrative, as Hull suggests, Jesus takes on disability for himself. He cannot see, and related to that is a temporary cognitive impairment: he does not know who it is that has hit him. He has moved from being a healer of the disabled, to one who starts from the perspective of the disabled, to one who is disabled.

It is in this context that the Cross should be set. Clearly, it is physically disabling. All too often we hear the language of suffering associated with disability. It is not however to be denied that with this disability comes painful suffering. With the physical disability goes cognitive impairment on – I choose these words carefully – a cosmic scale. We all have a deficit of understanding in relation to God, which puts those with or without cognitive impairment on the same level. When Jesus utters the cry 'My God, my God, why have you forsaken me?' we find God himself involved in that failure of understanding of himself. The humanist vision of the triumphant progress of human understanding is even beyond God himself.

---

27   Hull (2001), p. 157f.

LUKE 24:13–35

That very day two of them were going to a village named Emmaus, about seven miles from Jerusalem, and talking with each other about all these things that had happened. While they were talking and discussing together, Jesus himself drew near and went with them. But their eyes were kept from recognizing him. And he said to them, 'What is this conversation which you are holding with each other as you walk?' And they stood still, looking sad. Then one of them, named Cleopas, answered him, 'Are you the only visitor to Jerusalem who does not know the things that have happened there in these days?' And he said to them, 'What things?' And they said to him, 'Concerning Jesus of Nazareth, who was a prophet mighty in deed and word before God and all the people, and how our chief priests and rulers delivered him up to be condemned to death, and crucified him. But we had hoped that he was the one to redeem Israel. Yes, and besides all this, it is now the third day since this happened. Moreover, some women of our company amazed us. They were at the tomb early in the morning and did not find his body; and they came back saying that they had even seen a vision of angels, who said that he was alive. Some of those who were with us went to the tomb, and found it just as the women had said; but him they did not see.' And he said to them, 'O foolish men, and slow of heart to believe all that the prophets have spoken! Was it not necessary that the Christ should suffer these things and enter into his glory?' And beginning with Moses and all the prophets, he interpreted to them in all the Scriptures the things concerning himself. So they drew near to the village to which they were going. He appeared to be going further, but they constrained him, saying, 'Stay with us, for it is toward evening and the day is now far spent.' So he went in to stay with them. When he was at table with them, he took the bread and blessed, and broke it, and gave it to them. And their eyes were opened and they recognized him; and he vanished out of their sight. They said to each other, 'Did not our hearts burn within us while he talked to us on the road, while he opened to us the Scriptures?' And they rose that same hour and returned to Jerusalem; and they found the eleven gathered together and those who were with them, who said, 'The Lord has risen indeed, and has appeared to Simon!'

In this passage, Luke presents a paradigm of what it is to come to a faith in the resurrection. There is a deliberate contrast between Cleopas and his companion between the beginning and the end of the story. They begin by 'standing still, looking sad', and by the end their 'hearts are burning within' them, and they rise 'that same hour' and return to Jerusalem. They are energized. This process has been mediated in a number of ways: through talk, conversation, discourse; through text, that of Holy Scripture, and its verbal interpretation; through symbolic action, the sharing in a meal, which some would argue prefigures the Eucharist; through visual recognition. I have argued strongly that the theme of disability is central both to the ministry of Jesus, and to the passion narrative. Indeed it is the theme of disability which bears the burden of a considerable part of the narrative development from the ministry of Jesus to the crucifixion. If this is so, then our account of the resurrection and of Easter hope should be able to carry this theme forward. This passage from Luke shows how problematic this is, since all the ways in which resurrection faith is mediated – discourse, text, symbolic action, facial recognition – would be fundamentally inaccessible to Adam, as well as, to a greater or lesser extent, to many others with disabilities.

LUKE 24:36–39, 41–51

As they were saying this, Jesus himself stood among them. But they were startled and frightened, and supposed that they saw a spirit. And he said to them, 'Why are you troubled, and why do questionings rise in your hearts? See my hands and my feet, that it is I myself; handle me, and see; for a spirit has not flesh and bones as you see that I have.' [...] And while they still disbelieved for joy, and wondered, he said to them, 'Have you anything here to eat?' They gave him a piece of broiled fish, and he took it and ate before them. Then he said to them, 'These are my words which I spoke to you, while I was still with you, that everything written about me in the law of Moses and the prophets and the psalms must be fulfilled.' Then he opened their minds to understand the Scriptures, and said to them, 'Thus it is written, that the Christ should suffer and on the third day rise from the dead, and that repentance and forgiveness of sins should be preached in his name to all nations, beginning from Jerusalem. You are witnesses of these things. And behold, I send the promise of my Father upon you; but stay in the city, until you are clothed with power from on high.' Then he led them out as far as Bethany, and lifting up his hands he blessed them. While he blessed them, he parted from them, and was carried up into heaven.

Here Luke continues his account of the Resurrection, taking us forward to the Ascension. It is of key significance for the argument that the disabled Christ of the cross is recognized by his disabilities. We have seen how His identity is defined and given expression by His encounter with those with disabilities; here now it is disability which identifies Him: 'See my hands and my feet, that it is I myself.' However, in this Lucan account, there has been a change of theology. Luke omits, one might say censors, the great cry from the Cross 'My God, my God, why have you forsaken me', which marks, I have argued, a point of deep of identification both of Jesus, and (as Jesus reflects the situation of the whole of humanity) of the whole of humanity with those with learning disabilities. In place of that questioning cry as Jesus dies, we get the question of a risen Jesus: 'Why are you troubled and why do questionings arise in your hearts.' At very least, the totality of impairment which the scene of crucifixion represents has been subtlety modified by the Lucan presentation of the resurrection. Michel Foucault spoke of the power/knowledge doublet.[28] Here we see that doublet at work. Faith in the Resurrection, and the joy that flows from it, is predicated upon understanding, echoing the previous Emmaus story: 'He opened their minds to understand the Scriptures.' With knowledge goes power: 'Wait in the city, until you are clothed with power from on high.' It is thus important that as this narrative Christ's embodied wounds are a persistent presence: 'lifting up his hands he blessed them'. There is however a troubling ambiguity in the wounded Christ, who is now the enabled Christ, and who shows those wounds to others as a source of blessing.

From the foregoing, I hope that it is clear that I can very much affirm the words of Gene Robinson in his autobiography *In the Eye of the Storm*: 'I *love* the Bible. I owe my faith and life to the Bible and to its liberating message. It is in the Bible that I first met Jesus, and because of that when I see Jesus acting in my own life, I recognize him.' There

---

28   Cited in Moss (ed.) (1998), p. 175: 'the exercise of power itself creates and causes to emerge new objects of knowledge and accumulates new bodies of information' …'knowledge constantly induces effects of power.'

is one particular aspect of biblical teaching which Robinson recognizes and which unless it belonged to my own heart, life with Adam would have been unbearable: 'Scripture was the source of my belief that God loved me. Scripture was the source of my faith that – like the lepers and prostitutes and tax collectors and other outcasts – I too am included in God's embrace.'[29] However, Robinson then asks a concluding question which shows the starkness of having a biblical faith and living with a person who does not deal in words: 'Where would I be – where would any person of faith be – without the Bible?' It is not a question of choosing between my love for my son and a Scripture soaked spirituality. One learns to live with the tension, but that learning takes a long time.

In this chapter I have suggested that the capacity of Jesus to identify with people with disabilities and thence to approach the question of healing with a starting point in their identity rather than his own is a later development in his ministry. In this I have followed the synoptic tradition. However, in the Johannine tradition that development is much earlier in the question to the paralysed man at the pool at Bethzatha, who has been 'ill for thirty eight years'. To this man, whose disability is so much a part of his lifetime, Jesus addresses the question 'Do you want to be healed?'[30] For this man, it turns out that the major issue is that no-one will take him to the pool, and all get there before him, and this he tells to Jesus. The great difficulty is that Adam cannot tell me.

---

29 Robinson (2008), p. 61.
30 John 5:1–18.

CHAPTER 7

Liturgy

Belonging to the Catholic tradition within Anglicanism, the Eucharist is central to my spirituality. The Eucharist is not primarily, but importantly the place in which the relationship between a Christian priest and the local Christian community is both celebrated and worked out. As a member of the Christian Church, it is to participation in the Eucharist that I would have turned in order to wrestle with some of the problems which came to us as a family from caring for Adam. Some of the most memorable worship for me in the period between Adam's diagnosis and his eventual reception into full-time care occurred on those occasions when we were able to access respite care. I sometimes found myself, tired and anonymous, the member of the weekday congregation at a church far away from home, and praying with great intensity.

However, it was exactly the centrality which I would give to the Eucharist that caused me the greatest problems. As I came slowly to understand more about autism, I realized that it presented great challenges to the central act of worship within the Christian tradition to which I belonged and belong. In order to maintain my belonging to that community, I have had to approach some highly difficult issues in Eucharistic worship. I would not say that I have yet resolved those issues. Rather they have been absorbed into my spirituality.

The first and possibly the most significant of those issues was Adam's own participation within the worshipping community, and specifically within the Eucharist. The Christian Church in general has over recent years addressed issues of disability discrimination and access. One thinks in particular of the tremendously positive contribution of the charity *Through the Roof*.[1] However, despite the broad-based approach of *Through the Roof,* including, for example, on its website a guide to the inclusion of those with autistic spectrum disorders, church people in different denominations have tended to focus on the difficulties of providing access for wheelchairs. It is important that such difficulties should be overcome, but the overcoming of them can be a substitute for addressing the wider issues of the inclusion of those with all kinds of disabilities. The overall question which applies to worship is a reflection particularly of the issues to do with the education of those with disabilities: to what extent should those with disabilities be included within the mainstream, or to what extent should separate provision be made for them. Adam attends a school with a population of about 44 young people, from 11 to 19 years of age, with severe learning difficulties and associated challenging behaviour. About 75 per cent of the population of the school is on the autistic spectrum. One of the most memorable acts of worship which I have ever attended was a Harvest festival for the whole school in the local parish church shortly after his arrival there in 2005. The language was kept simple. Makaton signing[2] was available. Objects were used where possible rather than words. What was said and done was aimed at disabled people. As one of the congregation was my own son, it was ironic that I, as a 'non-disabled' person, felt more engaged than I do in many mainstream acts of worship. However, matters would be different if I was to take Adam to a mainstream act of worship. As far as I can tell Adam loves cathedrals: he seems to like the usually bright and open spaces, as bright and much more open than the spaces in which he usually finds himself. A few years ago on a visit to Llandaff Cathedral in Cardiff we found him uncharacteristically calmed, at least on that day, and indeed very much welcomed by members of the cathedral staff. That is his experience outside worship. It is an interesting question as to what kind of experience it would be for him, or for members of the congregation at solemn evensong when, unaware of

---

1   http://www.throughtheroof.org/ [accessed 25 October 2008].
2   Originally developed in the 1970s. See http://www.makaton.org [accessed 20 November 2008].

and indifferent to the protocols, he might cry out, flap his hands, jump on to the furniture, or run away through the congregation.

Shortly after his birth, Adam was baptized by Barry Morgan, then Bishop of Bangor. I would share the view of this expressed by Professor Frances Young in her theological reflections upon caring for her severely disabled son Arthur: 'It has always meant a great deal to me that Arthur is baptized. He will never be able to make his own response of faith, but his baptism as an infant means that he is a member of the body of Christ, and no-one can take that away from him or exclude him.'[3] Arthur's disability is different to that of Adam, but the force of the theological point is the same: through baptism, Adam is a full and Christ-accepted member of the Christian church, as full a member of that church as the Bishop (now Archbishop) who baptized him. In infant baptism, godparents take joint responsibility with the parents for the upbringing of the child in the Christian faith, as the child is not at that stage in his/her life able to express a commitment of faith. If we had used at Adam's baptism the contemporary Church of England order for baptism, rather than that of the Church in Wales, this is what would have been asked of his godparents and of us as his parents: 'In baptism this child begins his journey in faith. You speak for him today. Will you care for him and help him to take his place within the life and worship of Christ's church?' The parents and godparents reply: 'With the help of God we will.' Since Adam's baptism, as he has not developed articulate speech, there have been many occasions upon which I have had to speak on his behalf. This was among the first of many times. Of all the subjects upon which I have had to speak on Adam's behalf, speaking for him in his spiritual life is conceivably the most difficult. As we have seen, the task of caring for Adam presents enormous challenges both for us and for others. It could be said that *equally difficult* has been the task of helping him to take his place within the life and worship of Christ's church. All human beings change and develop from the moment of birth. Some humans either recognize within themselves, or have recognized by others, a parallel process of spiritual change and development. This spiritual process sometimes moves forward quite independently of the individual's progress through the human lifecycle, quite independently

---

3   Young (1998), p. 94.

of the individual's physical and mental development. Sometimes the two processes intersect: the individual's physical and mental development can bring about changes in his or her spiritual life: the individual's spiritual life can conversely impact upon mental and, perhaps to a lesser degree, physical development. Alongside the processes of physical and mental development Adam has running the development of his selfhood as a person with autism. His autism interacts with his physical and mental development. Alongside these processes, we have to consider what it means for Adam, from the day of his baptism, to begin and continue a journey in faith.

Integral to Christian initiation in the tradition to which I belong is the rite of confirmation. Edward Yarnold and J.D.C. Fisher in a contribution to *The Study of Liturgy* describe the evolution of the relationship between baptism and confirmation. In the first place, baptism and confirmation were part of a single act of liturgical initiation taking place during the preparations for Easter. The sequence within the Western rite was: baptism; anointing; presentation to the Bishop with laying on of hands; first communion during the Easter vigil.[4] Yarnold and Fisher describe how the laying on of hands by the Bishop became separated from the body of the rite of Christian initiation. In the first place this took place largely on the grounds that the Bishop was not necessarily immediately available:

> Hence confirmation was in actual practice coming more and more to be separated in time from baptism, and the interval was becoming longer; it was acquiring the appearance of an independent sacrament, and was no longer an indispensable preliminary to the receiving of communion. Thus the way was paved for the belief that confirmation is the sacrament of adolescents.[5]

In these circumstances, a twofold theology of confirmation has emerged, largely predicated in recent centuries on a division of opinion between Protestants and Catholics. A more Protestant view would see confirmation as a rite of adult commitment, subsequent to baptism. At the beginning of the Common Worship rite of confirmation, the Bishop asks the candidates:

---

4   The detail of this is set out in Jones, Wainwright, Yarnold (eds.), (1987), pp. 111–112.

5   Ibid., p. 115.

Have you been baptized in the name of the Father, and of the Son, and of the Holy Spirit? **I have.**

Are you ready with your own mouth and from your own heart to affirm your faith in Jesus Christ? **I am.**

Testimony by the candidates may follow.

A more Catholic view, without precluding the idea that those confirmed are called to respond to God's gift, would say that through the Bishop's laying on of hands the person confirmed is passively receiving the gifts of God's Holy Spirit. This is the prayer just before the laying on of hands in the Common Worship rite:

Almighty and ever-living God, you have given these your servants new birth in baptism by water and the Spirit, and have forgiven them all their sins. Let your Holy Spirit rest upon them: the Spirit of wisdom and understanding; the Spirit of counsel and inward strength; the Spirit of knowledge and true godliness; and let their delight be in the fear of the Lord. **Amen.**

Considering all these things, it can be imagined that the decision to ask for Adam to be confirmed was highly difficult. He could not and cannot make a commitment of faith, in the sense of being able to understand the content of that commitment, and expressing it in words. As this was the case, there were considerable ethical issues arising from asking him to take part in such a rite without his active consent. This was especially so as what happened to him in taking part in confirmation raised in such an acute way the nature of his disability. In what way was it meaningful for us to ask for God to give Adam wisdom, understanding, counsel, inward strength, knowledge, true Godliness and the fear of the Lord?

In taking the decision for Adam to be confirmed, our starting point has to be his own needs rather than our needs as a family or the requirements of the Church. That being said, the ways in which I reflected upon this had both a theological and a secular aspect. Confirmation, despite its long history as a separate rite, is intrinsically part of a single act of Christian initiation. I believe that his confirmation, just like his baptism, represented a moment of divine acceptance and inclusion. This issue can be approached from a secular direction, and especially from the consideration of the human rights of people with disabilities. Janet Read and Luke Clements, in their work *Disabled Children and the Law – research and good practice*, take as their starting point 'quality of life and human rights'. They describe their approach as being:

> founded on a very simple assumption. We believe that it should not be regarded as an exotic idea for disabled children and those close to them to aspire to a quality of life comparable to that enjoyed by others who do not live with disability [...] We should [...] never start from the assumption that an experience which is taken for granted by many non-disabled children and their families should be ruled out on the grounds of child being disabled. By contrast, if we start by assuming that disabled children and their families should have access to experiences which others routinely expect, the issue then becomes one of finding the route to achieve it and the services that will enable it to happen. To assume that disabled children and their families have the same basic social and human rights as other people is fundamental.[6]

Thus Adam's confirmation became the public expression, perhaps in an unspoken way, of a wider issue. I could not believe that we were right, simply on the grounds of his disability, to prevent him from experiencing something which, given the culture and beliefs of his family, would otherwise have happened. Indeed the event belonged to his human right to have access to the key elements of his own culture.

I will now describe the day of Adam's confirmation. At the time he was a pupil at Heronsbridge School in Bridgend in South Wales. As people with autism, and certainly Adam, rely upon consistency and stability, I felt that it was better that he should be confirmed in a space which was familiar to him, and that he, as far as we can be aware, associated with non-stressful experience. We therefore asked if it would be possible for us to use the soft play area of the school. It would also have been inappropriate for Adam to be confronted with a great number of unfamiliar people, so there was a small group of immediate family and friends, parents and godparents. Adam was not prepared for confirmation in the traditional way through confirmation classes. The service was necessarily short, including whatever was necessary

---

6   Read and Clements (2001), pp. 14–15.

of the Church in Wales' rite of confirmation. While wanting to ensure, obviously, that it was recognizably a service of confirmation, I felt that we should use as few words as possible. This goes back to taking Adam himself as our starting point. I did not want to surround him with an accumulation of – to him – incomprehensible language. There were two readings, deliberately chosen. The first was 1 Corinthians 13, chosen to allow us to reflect upon the relationship between speech, (dis)ability and the work of care: 'If I speak in the tongues of men and of angels, but have not love, I am a noisy gong or a clanging cymbal. And if I have prophetic powers, and understand all mysteries and all knowledge, and if I have all faith, so as to remove mountains, but have not love, I am nothing. If I give away all I have, and if I deliver my body to be burned, but have not love, I gain nothing.' In his peroration St. Paul looks forward to the end-time: 'Now I know in part; then I shall understand fully, even as I have been fully understood.' One of many things that were happening on that day is that others – church, family, and friends – were being helped to understand Adam. As a learning disabled person he has challenges in understanding: those are equalled by the challenges that others have in understanding him. The starting point of understanding is unqualified acceptance. The Gospel reading was Mark's description of Jesus accepting and blessing children.

Some time elapsed between Adam's confirmation and his first communion, and I suspect in retrospect that this happened not by accident, but rather because there was a need for a time to assimilate the theological and other implications of his confirmation. We are very fortunate than even though Adam lives some distance away from us – just under three hours journey – there are occasions when his carers bring him on a home visit. One Sunday he arrived in Llangeler just before lunch. I had arranged that the final service that day would take place in the smallest of my five churches, and with a specially simplified communion service, while including all – but no more than – that was necessary for this to be a valid celebration of the Eucharist. At about three o'clock we set off in convoy. I was pleased to see a number of my parishioners with us in loving support. I can guess that this may have been for some of them the first occasion upon which they had met a teenager with severe autism and attention deficit hyperactivity disorder, let alone reflected on the place of that person within the liturgical community. It is not true of any of the churches within my parish, but it is well known that there are some congregations in which children and teenagers are not made overwhelmingly welcome, let alone those with extreme disabilities.[7] Adam uses one word both in order to indicate that he wants to relieve himself or to indicate that he really quite urgently wants to be elsewhere, especially when his autistic need for consistency is disrupted by finding himself in unfamiliar circumstances. I was not therefore totally reassured as I began the service to hear him cry in a loud voice: 'Toilet!' The particular reason for my concern was that, at that point in the service, I did not know whether it was appropriate to give him communion. Adam does not give many signs of consent one way or another and so this more than slight indication that he did not want to be there weighed more heavily than usual.

We came to the communion itself. There was an overwhelming sense of usualness about the way in which the row of communicants came forward and knelt at the altar. Alongside them, Adam's two carers brought him forward. I had told them that if for any reason giving communion to Adam was practically difficult, then I would – of course – not persist. His mere presence was special enough. As I moved down the line with the chalice, Adam looked up, saw me, and shouted 'It's a cup!' Without sentimentality, and without reading into the occasion more than is appropriate, I took that to be the response by which Adam affirmed his own liturgical participation. To take it another way, we could say that this was an affirmation of the emptiness of the occasion: what Adam saw was a cup, and nothing more than a cup. What happened on that day belongs to the complexities of the relationship of the sacred and the secular which this book explores; the possibility and the necessity of transcending that relationship.

---

7   I am mindful of the complexities of a case in Bertha, Minnesota, in which the parish priest sought an restraining order upon a family to prevent them from bringing their son – co-incidentally also called Adam – to Mass. The family found a spiritual home, and a greater welcome in a neighbouring parish. Reported by ABC news in May 2008. http://abcnews.go.com/TheLaw/Story?id=4885322 [accessed 22 February 2008]. This is not to make comment on the issues of this particular story but only to note its presence on the record.

Having discussed Adam's place within the liturgical community, I shall now imagine that I am attending the Eucharist, as the parent of a child on the autistic spectrum. What follows is a commentary upon the Eucharist, in which I share a response to the action of the Eucharist, both as intellectual and affective response. I am trying to describe both ideas and emotions, to describe the spirituality which emerges from living in family-community with a person with autism. Again, I have chosen to use the text of the Common Worship of the Church of England, although much of what I have to say would be applicable in general to any Eucharistic text. Much controversy down the years has gone into the language of the Eucharist: Latin or the vernacular, and if in the vernacular should the language be archaic or contemporary. Within multilingual and multicultural contexts here with us in Wales, in Europe, there are controversies as to which of the local languages should be used for the local liturgy, reflecting not so much liturgical priorities as the necessary struggles between different communities. These are highly significant controversies. However, like so much else, they have been set within a certain perspective by living with a non-lingual person. In one way, that experience has taught me that liturgy should, almost above all, communicate: if we have the gift of communication we should use it, rather than, for whatever reason, including stubborn liturgical conservatism, turning our back upon it. Yet, this is merely 'almost above all': there is something deeper and higher than communication itself.

The president may say

In the name of the Father, and of the Son, and of the Holy Spirit.

All

Amen.

The Trinitarian formula of the introduction stamps the act of worship as unmistakeably Christian. Christian reflection upon the Holy Trinity has continued since the earliest times. As is well known, one of the fundamental problems which has to be addressed is how to reconcile unity and trinity, oneness and threeness, how to speak of three persons in God, while preserving a monotheistic faith. A way in which this problem has been addressed is to speak of Trinity and community. In this model, human community comes to be modelled upon the divine community: a community which seeks the perfection of God maintains its fundamental unity while acknowledging diversity, and the integrity of the discreet persons with it. Archbishop Rowan Williams places this way of thinking at the heart of soteriology. For him, the Incarnation is:

> ...the bridge between human and divine society, the revelation of how human community is rooted in the communal existence of Father, Son and Holy Spirit. The logic needs a little teasing out, but it will bear examination.[8] A divine person, constituted by the completely reciprocal and selfless relations of God as Trinity, comes to act and live as a human person; thus, where this person is concerned, there is possible a different level, a different depth of human relation than would be the case with any other. As we are reconstituted by relationship with Christ, our capacity for relationship with each other is naturally changed as well.[9]

As a way of approaching the relationship between the things of God and that which belongs to secular community, this model has been, and will without doubt continue to be, extremely fruitful. Nobody would say that any model of the Trinity provides an exhaustive description of the divine nature. However, if we take this model to be determinative, we are in peril of excluding those who – by their own essential nature – find life in community to be problematic. Even if Adam could grasp the literal sense of the words in which this model is expressed, we may presume that he would find the model, in itself, baffling, rooted as it is in reciprocal relationships both human and divine. This matter is further complicated by the thinking of Jean Vanier. For Vanier, 'community' represents, in practical terms, a means of overcoming the marginality of those with learning disabilities. He speaks of the L'Arche communities which, under his founding inspiration, have done such groundbreaking work for and with those with learning disabilities:

---

8   See pp. 70 and 101 for the whole question of the place of logic and reason within spirituality.

9   Williams (2000), p. 226. The chapter from which this is taken is dedicated to the discussion of 'Incarnation and the renewal of community'.

> L'Arche is special, in the sense that we are trying to live in commu-
> nity with people who are mentally handicapped... The particular
> suffering of the person who is mentally handicapped, as of all mar-
> ginal people, is a feeling of being excluded, worthless and unloved.
> It is through everyday life in community and the love that must be
> incarnate in this, that handicapped people can begin to discover
> that they have a value, that they are loved and so are lovable.[10]

I have already touched on the question of what it means to say that
Adam 'suffers'.[11] Vanier takes as his starting point the suffering of
those with learning disabilities, and from this starting point, he considers the difference that is wrought by life in community, in terms
of affective and cognitive response: 'feeling', what it is to 'discover'
value in oneself. Such a cognitive and affective response may well
not be within Adam's range. This book is, amongst other things, a
reflection upon God, and the experience of living with a person with
a learning disability: the problematic of community belongs in both
relationships.

THE GREETING

The president greets the people

The Lord be with you **and also with you.** *(or)*

Grace, mercy and peace from God our Father and the Lord Jesus
Christ be with you **and also with you.**

The priest turns from a contemplation of the reciprocal relations which
subsist within the Godhead to the establishment of a reciprocal relationship with the local Christian community. It will already be evident
that the reciprocity implied in the response 'and also with you' does
not belong to Adam's way of being.

That same way of being challenges also the use of the three key
terms – grace, mercy and peace. The whole edifice of the relationship
between Catholic and Protestant Christianity is based upon differing
interpretations of God's grace. At the risk of caricature, the Protestant

---

10   Vanier (2007), p. 11.
11   See p. 67.

insight, if it may be called such, was to give a priority to give God's grace, as opposed to good works. The fundamental question of salvation was for each individual in the kind and quality of her/his response to that grace. Adam's way of being once more stands outside such reciprocity. However, we must also see here the force of what is, within the historic debate on grace, one of the key Pauline scriptural texts: 'By the grace of God, I am what I am, and his grace towards me was not in vain.'[12] If we say that the being as such of an individual is, or can be, constituted by grace, we need to ask the question of how that process works in the case of Adam.

The term mercy carries with it the sense of compassion, and of abstaining from anger and judgement, be that anger and judgement either righteous or unrighteous. Compassion involves an understanding that the person to whom one is compassionate has a mind which functions in the same way as oneself. Divine compassion is predicated upon the Incarnation: that God has been within the skin of, or more colloquially, 'in the shoes of', humanity. As it happens, I have never found Adam to be unkind: for him anger and judgement, and the abstaining from them, belong to a reciprocity which is not his.

The sense in which Adam does, or could potentially, enjoy peace is difficult to ascertain. Because of his attention deficit hyperactivity disorder, he is experienced by others as someone who is never at rest. Because of his autism, he is constantly seeking to satisfy his need for engagement with those things with which he is obsessed, including coils, wires and tubes. When he cannot satisfy these needs he can become tearful and distressed. As he has so little expressive language, he is sometimes tearful for no apparent reason. In one way, it is exactly those autistic obsessions which constitute for him his joy and his peace. As peace is here described as gift, Adam experiences those things which are the target of his obsessions as gift, as given to him.

From Easter Day to Pentecost this acclamation follows

Alleluia. Christ is risen. **He is risen indeed. Alleluia.**

Wittgenstein at the beginning of *Philosophical Investigations II* asks poignantly: 'Can only those hope who can talk? Only those who have

---

12   1 Corinthians 15:10.

mastered the use of a language. That is to say, the phenomena of hope are modes of this complicated form of life. (If a concept refers to a character of human handwriting, it has not application to beings that do not write.)[13] It is said to be characteristically human to be aware from our earliest years of our own finitude, or death. The thought is there in the Letter to the Hebrews: 'all those who through fear of death were subject to lifelong bondage'.[14] Upon that awareness, and upon the release from that fear, the central Christian proclamation of the resurrection is predicated. Adam by his very nature has been – as far as we can tell – exempted from that awareness and the concomitant fear. He is in one sense distanced from the central Christian proclamation, and in another closer to it than most of us will ever get to experience. A parting can be described as a 'little death': it is not clear how Adam experiences parting except to say that he does not experience it as many others do.

Related to this is Adam's sense of time. He cannot tell the time; he does not tell the time to others. One may doubt whether he has a concept of time. Into the observance of the chronological patterns of daily life we are ritualized by socialization. The capitalist economy functions – insofar as it functions – because workers sell quantified amounts of time to their employers. We internalize this from those around us. Adam does not have that socialization, that capacity to internalize from the models which others give him. Owing to the necessarily highly structured nature of his education, and indeed of his day-to-day life, he will have a sense if not of time rather of succession, of one activity following upon another. People with autism are said to be comfortable with structure. I do not doubt this, but sometimes suspect that the structure which is imposed upon the lives of people with autism may well benefit us time-bound people as much as people with autism. As Adam has no interest in watching a clock, he may be said already to dwell within eternity.

Words of welcome or introduction may be said.

Prayer of Preparation *This prayer may be said*

---

13   Wittgenstein (2001), p. 148.
14   Hebrews 2:15.

Almighty God, to whom all hearts are open, all desires known, and from whom no secrets are hidden: cleanse the thoughts of our hearts by the inspiration of your Holy Spirit, that we may perfectly love you, and worthily magnify your holy name; through Christ our Lord. Amen.

We only have immediate access to our own being, our own desires. All other humans are to some extent mysterious, and reveal themselves to us to a greater or lesser extent. We can never be totally certain that this revelation of other selves as it presents itself to us is fundamentally trustworthy. On account of his challenges with language, and with reciprocal social interaction, Adam is prevented from making that revelation of his 'inner' self, either honestly or otherwise. His selfhood remains fundamentally mysterious: this prayer postulates that that selfhood, in common with the selfhood of all, is immediately known to God.

The work of the Holy Spirit is described in various ways in the New Testament. The account of the day of Pentecost in the Book of Acts provides a paradigm for that action in the enabling of expressive language, and in the shared understanding of language: 'And they were all filled with the Holy Spirit and began to speak in other tongues, as the Spirit gave them utterance'; 'And they were amazed and wondered, saying, "Are not all these who are speaking Galileans? And how is it that we hear, each of us in his own native language?"' Adam uses language, but only the most basic of expressive language. He does not engage in conversation for its own sake.

Language essentially involves the naming of individuals and things. In order to glorify, to magnify God, we need to give name to him. Adam has enough language to name different things. As he uses language to express his most immediate concrete needs, these words tend to refer to things within his immediate physical environment. I have never heard him use the word 'God', as God does not present to him in his immediate physical environment. As St. John's Gospel reminds us, nobody has ever seen God.

PRAYERS OF PENITENCE

> Our Lord Jesus Christ said: The first commandment is this: 'Hear, O Israel, the Lord our God is the only Lord. You shall love the Lord your God with all your heart, with all your soul, with all your mind, and with all your strength.'
>
> The second is this: 'Love your neighbour as yourself.' There is no other commandment greater than these. On these two commandments hang all the law and the prophets. **Amen. Lord, have mercy.**[15]

The Christian Church has encountered and does encounter problems when it seeks to move the ethical agenda away from the twofold summary of the Old Testament law. Within a strictly orthodox Christianity in ways which are not often recognized there exists a kind of moral relativism: no other ethical demands, no specific regulation of particular moral issues can claim the absolute nature of the twofold command of love for God and love for one's neighbour: 'There is no other commandment greater than these. On these two commandments hang all the law and the prophets.' Our ethics can be taken as being derived from existing, inherited moral and social codes – the law – as well as from a vision of the way our society can be – the prophets. No aspect of our ethical inheritance or of our ethical vision can be taken as having greater force than the twofold commandment of love. The reciprocal loving relationship between God and humanity becomes central to the making of community, and to the ethic by which behaviours within that community are governed and measured: 'we love because He first loved us'.

The statements which I have made here clearly belong to a wider ethical debate which is significant both inside and outside the Church.[16] While in no sense retracting the critical force of those statements within the wider debate, it is difficult to see where Adam's way of life sits within such a view of ethics. He is clearly someone who is loved, but because of the deficits within his social skills he cannot easily involve himself in reciprocal loving relationships. When he was a young boy, he did not engage in cuddling, and would certainly not

---

15   1 John 4:19.
16   See Chapter 9.

initiate such a contact. Those of us who would argue, as Christians would argue, that our being in Christ marks God's creation of an new community, of a new way of relating between human beings, have to be challenged by one for whom being in community is not significant for his self-awareness.

> God so loved the world that he gave his only Son Jesus Christ to save us from our sins, to be our advocate in heaven, and to bring us to eternal life.

The Christian churches sometimes give the impression that God's love is specially shown to those who belong to the community of faith. It should be noted here that, following the text from St. John's Gospel, the starting point of salvation is God's love for the world, and thence for all those in the world: able and disabled, included and excluded, those of my language, your language, and no language, those of your nation and my nation. God's love is for all – the Christian community is constituted by those who respond to the divine initiative of love. Within the Christian community we have ways of normalizing that response and the consequent ways of belonging to the community in order to make the response and the belonging recognizable both to those within and to those outside the community. I am thinking here particularly of the liturgies of baptism and confirmation. We need to give some serious and new thought to how those who are either not able to vocalize or otherwise able to articulate that response can be and should be included within local Christian communities. Those who are not able to make articulate response, those who for whatever reason find expressive language difficult, belong to a very much wider category than those with autistic spectrum disorders. By reflecting on how those who have autistic spectrum disorder can genuinely and fully be involved within the Christian community, we are addressing a much wider issue in relation to Christian mission.

Once we seek to coalesce the secular sense and the theological sense of the word 'advocate' then there are some highly interesting consequences. One would not in any way wish to identify sin and disability. The story, for example, of the healing of the paralytic in Mark 2 has been read in exactly this way, with the words of healing heard as the announcement of forgiveness. Persons with disability or disabilities will make a range of response to their own healing, and indeed to the occasions when their disability is medicalized and therefore taken as being the target of healing strategies. However, we can turn all of this upon its head, by saying that all people are disabled, in the sense that sin, as a turning away from the will of God – who as almighty is taken to be without disability – dramatically limits our human capacity. Thence, in common with many people with disabilities, especially those who do not access reason or articulate speech, we are in need of an advocate, who is alongside us in our experience, and speaks powerfully on our behalf. Jesus' advocacy consists of the healer of Mark 2[17] becoming the disabled body on the cross.

> Let us confess our sins in penitence and faith, firmly resolved to keep God's commandments and to live in love and peace with all.
>
> *All* **Almighty God, our heavenly Father, we have sinned against you and against our neighbour in thought and word and deed, through negligence, through weakness, through our own deliberate fault. We are truly sorry and repent of all our sins. For the sake of your Son Jesus Christ, who died for us, forgive us all that is past and grant that we may serve you in newness of life to the glory of your name. Amen.**
>
> *The president says* Almighty God, who forgives all who truly repent, have mercy upon you, pardon and deliver you from all your sins, confirm and strengthen you in all goodness, and keep you in life eternal; through Jesus Christ our Lord. All **Amen.**

I am writing this with a deliberate awareness of the implications of what I am saying, and with no sentimentality whatsoever, but, to the best of my recollection, I cannot remember an occasion upon which Adam has wilfully sought to do that which is wrong rather than that which is right. Apart from anything else, in order to make that choice he would have to articulate it in language, at a level of abstraction which his linguistic capacity does not permit. The furthest that I would be prepared to go would be to say that Adam thinks strategically, in that, for example, if he were intending to leave a room he would wait until a carer was not in the way of his exit, or observing him. Adam in common with many autistic people has tearful tantrums when he is not able to pursue one of his obsessions. One of the greatest difficulties

---

17   See Chapter 6.

in raising awareness of autism among the general public is explaining that these autistic tantrums in no way constitute bad behaviour in the sense that our wider society understands it. It is Adam's autism which presents itself, and not a failure of his self control or indeed a failure to control him. There are many people with higher functioning autism or Asperger Syndrome who end up as the victims of a legal system which fails to distinguish between the presenting effects of disability and criminality. It is most important that people with autism do not become caught up in a misapplication of God's own legal code. I would not say that all people with autism and Asperger Syndrome are innocent. Owing to the position that Adam occupies on the autistic spectrum, I would say that he – very nearly – is. I chose to use the phrase 'very nearly' because this would otherwise compromise a fundamental *a priori* of soteriology, that Christ is 'like unto us in all ways, except that he did not sin', and thus able to bring salvation to sinful humanity.

> **Glory to God in the highest, and peace to his people on earth. Lord God, heavenly King, almighty God and Father, we worship you, we give you thanks, we praise you for your glory. Lord Jesus Christ, only Son of the Father, Lord God, Lamb of God, you take away the sin of the world: have mercy on us; you are seated at the right hand of the Father: receive our prayer. For you alone are the Holy One, you alone are the Lord, you alone are the Most High, Jesus Christ, with the Holy Spirit, in the glory of God the Father. Amen.**

Peter G. Cobb in his article on *The Liturgy of the Word in the Early Church* – a contribution to the collection *The Study of Liturgy* described the origin of the *Gloria in Excelsis*:

> This is one of the few surviving *psalmi idiotici*, popular hymns modelled on the Psalms and Canticles, of which *Phos Hilarion* ['O gladsome light'] is another [...] It could [...] be the case that the *Gloria in Excelsis* is really part of the Morning Office which was commonly celebrated immediately before Mass, but according to a not improbable tradition, it was first used by the Pope at the Christmas Midnight Mass, and its use was extended to Sunday's and feasts by Pope Symmachus (498–514). For several centuries its

use at Mass was a privilege confined to bishops. [….] In the seventh century, a priest could sing it, but only at Easter.[18]

The word 'idiot' has all kinds of negative resonances for people with learning disabilities and those who care for them. Liddell and Scott's Greek-English Lexicon denoted the range of meanings within the orginal Greek. To summarize: it can mean a private person, an individual as opposed to the State, one in a private station, as opposed to holding public office or taking part in public affairs, a common man, one without professional or other knowledge, unskilled, an average person, as opposed to a person. Finally, it can denote someone who originates from the same country as oneself. If it means any or all of these things, then to have such a song located at the heart of Christian liturgy is of supreme importance. Equally, the historic fact that the liturgical performance of this song was for a long historical period was monopolized by one who was engaged in public affairs, literate, and of high status has a significance which cannot be underrated.

THE COLLECT

The Collect is a set prayer for a particular Sunday in the year, which will therefore not simply be used in a given local church, but in other churches of the same denomination. One of its functions is to ensure that the local congregation is aware of joining in, on any given Sunday, with the wider prayer of the church. The local congregation is implicitly called upon to imagine other congregations at prayer. The recognition is that local congregational experience is of importance, but it is not to be absolutized as the only experience. The whole idea depends upon an imaginative recreation of the experience of others, who are absent. As we have already seen, Adam has enormous difficulty with imaginatively recreating and thence sharing in the experience of others. Moreover we are not clear that those people and things which are absent to him are considered by him to be real. There is also the question of the extent to which he recalls those who are absent.

---

18   Jones, *et al.* (1978), p. 183.

SCRIPTURE READINGS

I have already considered in Chapter 6 how the use of Scripture sits within the overall framework of thought of this book. In the liturgical reading of Scripture before a congregation, we are confronted with the question of the shared understanding of Scripture. The question with which this confronts Anglican Christians is the content of our interpretation: how we can worship together when we understand different things of the same scriptural passage. Maybe the real question is of our capacity for interpretation: how we can worship together when there are within the worshipping group varieties of capacity to interpret.

For the purposes of this chapter, I have taken a Eucharistic prayer almost at random from Common Worship; it is Eucharistic prayer G.

The Lord be with you **and also with you.**

Lift up your hearts. **We lift them to the Lord.**

Let us give thanks to the Lord our God. **It is right to give thanks and praise.**

Blessed are you, Lord God, our light and our salvation; to you be glory and praise for ever. From the beginning you have created all things and all your works echo the silent music of your praise. In the fullness of time you made us in your image, the crown of all creation. You give us breath and speech, that with angels and archangels and all the powers of heaven we may find a voice to sing your praise: **Holy, holy, holy Lord, God of power and might, heaven and earth are full of your glory. Hosanna in the highest. Blessed is he who comes in the name of the Lord. Hosanna in the highest.**

Even when it is juxtaposed with the 'silent music of...praise', there is a sense here that speech is a universal gift – a given. The transcendent significance of a lack of speech is indicated by the purpose of speech, which is, with those on earth and in heaven, to sing the praises of God.

How wonderful the work of your hands, O Lord. As a mother tenderly gathers her children, you embraced a people as your own.

When they turned away and rebelled your love remained steadfast. From them you raised up Jesus our Saviour, born of Mary, to be the living bread, in whom all our hungers are satisfied. He offered his life for sinners, and with a love stronger than death he opened wide his arms on the cross.

The giving and receiving of care stand at the heart of the story of salvation. It culminates in the moment of unconditional inclusion upon the cross, when Christ opens wide his arms. There stands a danger of postulating in the spiritual realm the meeting of all need – 'Jesus our Saviour...in whom all our hungers are satisfied'; this can be the psychological and spiritual compensation for the failure to meet need in the realm of the everyday. The meeting of spiritual need and the failure to meet social need certainly stand in ironic juxtaposition.

On the night before he died, he came to supper with his friends and, taking bread, he gave you thanks. He broke it and gave it to them, saying: Take, eat; this is my body which is given for you; do this in remembrance of me. At the end of supper, taking the cup of wine, he gave you thanks, and said: Drink this, all of you; this is my blood of the new covenant, which is shed for you and for many for the forgiveness of sins. Do this, as often as you drink it, in remembrance of me.

Lord, by your cross and resurrection you have set us free. You are the Saviour of the world.

Father, we plead with confidence his sacrifice made once for all upon the cross; we remember his dying and rising in glory, and we rejoice that he intercedes for us at your right hand. Pour out your Holy Spirit as we bring before you these gifts of your creation; may they be for us the body and blood of your dear Son. As we eat and drink these holy things in your presence, form us in the likeness of Christ, and build us into a living temple to your glory.

Bring us at the last with [N and] all the saints to the vision of that eternal splendour for which you have created us; through Jesus Christ, our Lord, by whom, with whom, and in whom, with all who stand before you in earth and heaven, we worship you, Father almighty, in songs of everlasting praise: **Blessing and honour and glory and power be yours for ever and ever. Amen.**

Christ's words of institution at the Last Supper, and their interpretation, lie at the heart of the faultline which has divided Christianity since the Reformation. A Catholic would stress the literal sense of the words: the bread is literally the body of Christ; the wine is literally His blood. A Protestant would want to see this as a memorial meal, calling to mind the salvific event of the Cross. This is the theological background of the words: 'his sacrifice made once for all upon the cross'. Subsequent liberal thought would wish to think of the 'beyond in the midst', the bread and wine bringing the mystery of that which is beyond us into the heart of the liturgical community. It was this thinking which had priests turn away from an Eastward facing position, turned with their congregations to the beyond, to a Westward facing position, facing the congregations, those communities among whom the beyond became a present realm. As we have seen, Adam would have difficulties with any interpretation which speaks of the social and the communal. We may suspect that he would have difficulties with recollection and memory. A person on the autistic spectrum who has the capacity for speech, or a person with Asperger Syndrome, can have a very literal sense of the use of speech: if bread is called body, then body it is, without symbolic remainder. We may suspect that Adam would – if only we could ask him – be most comfortable with the Catholic interpretation, but it should be said that this comfort would arise directly from his disability. It may well be that for all of us our doctrine should arise from our disability, whatever that disability may be.

The service continues with the Lord's Prayer.

Our Father who art in heaven

We have already examined in Chapter 5 the immediacy of the physical for Adam, and the consequent difficulties once we postulate, as we do as Christians, a non-physical transcendent, 'supernatural' realm.

Hallowed be thy name,

Worship is here predicated upon the capacity to utter the name of God.

thy kingdom come, thy will be done, on earth as it is in heaven

I would want to insist emphatically, in ways which we will further examine in the following chapter, that Christianity is programmatically committed to a reshaping of the political order, interpreted in the term 'the kingdom of God'. We are equally committed to the sense that this is a realizable goal, within the sphere of the secular, that it will be 'on earth as it is in heaven'. Experiencing life with Adam sent me away from any belief that the term 'kingdom of God' is a purely spiritual term, evacuated of any political meaning; yet Adam could not conceptualize the visible/invisible – already/not yet which forms the concept of the kingdom of God.

Give us this day our daily bread

Adam will never be economically active. He is radically dependent upon the work of others for his food, shelter and clothing. The prayer here suggests that we all share that contingency, however much that may be hidden by the workings of the market economy within the plenty of Western societies.

And forgive us our trespasses, as we forgive those who trespass against us.

It can be imagined that under the pressures described in Chapter 2, finding the capacity to forgive has on occasions been extremely difficult. One might suggest that its difficulty is such that it only comes by prayer. Conversely, one of the initial reactions of many parents and carers when a loved one is diagnosed as being on the autistic spectrum is guilt: is it something that I have done wrong? Even when those initial feelings have been thought through, and recognized for what they are, a sense of guilt still clings to us, even when it no longer has a basis.

And lead us not into temptation, but deliver us from evil.

In some translations, we ask to be delivered from 'the time of trial'. From my earliest years, I have prayed that prayer, and it was not answered. The very fact that we pray the prayer indicates that it is not always answered: that we live in a world in which times of trial do come.

BLESSING

I have already discussed the question of the ambiguity of God's blessing. After the blessing the priest says: 'Go in peace to love and serve the Lord' and the congregation replies 'In the name of Christ, Amen.' I work as a priest to urge people to come to church, that they may go from there with a renewed sense of personal and shared peace. The peace that I get is from having been in a place in which my most ultimate concerns are raised with a fresh intensity. Some of the liturgical and doctrinal arguments about the Eucharist/Mass/Communion, which are reflected in its many names, hardly get close to showing its wonder.

CHAPTER 8

The State We Are In

This chapter which is concerned with political theology, and the following final chapter 'The Transformation of the Church', which is concerned with the rather different subject of contemporary ecclesiastical politics, sit alongside each other. The question which is addressed is this: if we acknowledge the simple existence of autism, and allow that existence to transform our understanding of the Western tradition of thought, in the ways which have been outlined, what then are the consequences for the practical issues in the life of the Church and the State? The earlier chapter, in which I described the changes brought about in our family by life with Adam, by the simple fact of Adam's existence, represented a great 'change of mind'. I would not want to overinterpret, because interpretation can obscure the experience itself, and I certainly would not want through interpretation to make the experience sound grander than it actually was. Grand it was not. However, needing to grasp what was actually happening, I did turn once more to the thought of Michel Foucault. Foucault, when reflecting upon history, which is, after all, only made up of a myriad of personal accounts, just like my own, wanted to speak not of continuity but of discontinuity, and of what he called 'epistemic break'. Repeating my own warning about overinterpretation, I do believe that what I went through was exactly an 'epistemic break', in which older ways of handling reality became inadequate for their task. The question which Foucault asks is of the conditions in which new discourse arises from older, original discourse. The question which we should now ask is whether we can identify in our contemporary religious and political discourse, the conditions under which new discourse can arise. Given the overall framework of this book, I am hinting that that new discourse may well – ironically – originate from the irrational and/or the unspoken. We may well – whether we like it or not – be about to encounter a decisive rupture both in our religious and political discourse, in a single movement which transcends the boundary between the sacred and the secular.

The experience with Adam brought me, as a Christian priest, into an inevitably close contact with contemporary political systems, particularly those concerned with the delivery of public services in health, education and social care. This chapter offers a conjoint political and theological reflection upon those systems. The conjoint nature of the reflection is just one aspect of the redrawing of the relationship between the sacred and the secular which is among my chief themes. Although Adam's life and his daily wellbeing is radically influenced by the success or otherwise of political systems, Adam does not get to participate in the political process. In March 2005, Chris Sear of the Parliament and Constitution Centre produced a briefing note for the House of Commons Library entitled *Electoral Franchise – Who can vote?* In section B of this short document, Sear provides a list for a general election of 'legal incapacities to vote'. This list for example includes 'anyone under 18 years old on polling day', and 'Members of the House of Lords, including life peers, Church of England archbishops and bishops and hereditary peers who have retained their seat in the House of Lords... Convicted persons detained in pursuance of their sentences [...] This includes offenders detained in mental hospitals.' As Anne Borsay notes, mental health patients, other than those with a criminal record, are now allowed to vote.[1] Sear adds one last category to his list: 'Under common law, people with mental disabilities if, on polling day, they are incapable of making a reasoned judgement.'[2] The specific grounds on which Adam is excluded from political process is based on the nature of reason itself. Within the Western tradition democratic institutions and our thinking about the capacity of reason have developed in tandem: part of the purpose of

---

1   Borsay (2005), p. 282. For a fuller exploration of Anne Borsay's work in disability history, see further in this chapter, p. 157–8.
2   Sear (2005), p. 5. Accessed 5 January 2010.

this book has been to hold reason up to critical scrutiny from a theological and philosophical perspective. Adam would not understand a polling station, a political party, or a cross. If he cannot access politics in that way, the question that I pose is in what other ways should he be enabled to do so? The answer requires some imagination, and I am not saying that I have the answer. As people like Adam are normally hidden away in a variety of residential settings, there is no pressure for that imagination to be exercised.

The starting point of political theology is contemporary context. In order to ascertain where we are now, it is necessary to look at where we have been, so in the first place I offer a selective and by no means exhaustive history of the provision of public care for those with disabilities. There are a number of fascinating studies of the place of the 'fool' in medieval society.[3] The fundamental point is that those with some kind of learning disability found support with the social structures of the court. The tradition of the courtly fool is of someone who speaks truth to power, because he does not know the consequences of that speech. One may guess that some of those called fools were those with Asperger Syndrome, loquacious, intellectually able, but unable to see the social niceties which in a highly ritualized society would be violated by what they had to say. On the other hand, it is exactly that high level of ritualization which would be appreciated by a person with autistic spectrum disorder. The tradition of the 'courtly fool' showed a surprising persistence in the serious mindedness of the post-Reformation period, through Elizabeth I's Will Somers, through to Archie Armstrong in the courts both of James I and Charles I. Archie was excluded from court when, on the failure of Archbishop Laud's attempt to introduce the new prayer book in Scotland in 1638, he commented: 'Whoe's feule now? Does not your grace her [sic] the news from Striveling [Stirling, also "place of strife"]?'[4] The Archbishop complained to his fellow councillors, and Archie's exile marked, according

3   See, among much else: Enid Welsford, *The Fool – His Social and Literary History*, Faber & Faber, 1935; John Southworth, *Fools and Jesters at the English Court* Sutton, 1998; and Beatrice K. Otto, *Fools are Everywhere – the court jester around the world*, University Press, Chicago, 2001.

4   R. Malcolm Smuts, 'Armstrong, Archibald (d. 1672)', *Oxford Dictionary of National Biography*, Oxford University Press, September 2004; online edn, January 2008 [http://www.oxforddnb.com/view/article/653, accessed 28 July 2008, subscription necessary].

to his entry in the Dictionary of National Biography, the end to an honourable tradition: 'Although Armstrong's position as court jester was quickly filled after his dismissal by a man named Muckle John, this successor failed to achieve much notoriety, and the role of court fool died out after the civil war.'[5]

In her book *Disability and Social Policy in Britain Since 1750*, Anne Borsay takes up the story, and shows the ways in which the State (rather than the royal court) has exercised its caring role. It is a story which is of a piece with Foucault's account of the *grande enfermement*: those with learning disabilities came to be no longer within the public sphere of the court, but to be confined within much more private spaces. Archie Armstrong had a voice, which was heard by not only James I and Charles I, but even by the King of Spain, who granted him a pension.[6] Much of disability's subsequent history is undocumented, because it belonged to those who were – actually and/or metaphorically – voiceless. The trace which disability leaves in the documentary record arises because of the efforts of the State simultaneously to care and to control. Reading Borsay's book, it does not require a great effort of imagination to grasp how things would have been for Adam if he had been born two centuries ago. He may well have found himself within the workhouse:

> The 1834 Act [The Poor Law Amendment Act] defined the workhouse as a staging post for 'dangerous lunatics' *en route* for specialized asylums, but requiring their removal after no more than two weeks. Those with 'harmless' mental impairments on the other hand, were allowed to reside on a long term basis. A shortage of asylum places, allied to the reluctance of the guardians to meet their higher marginal costs, meant that not all inmates with serious mental illnesses or disruptive behaviour patterns were transferred.[7]

Borsay records that by local initiative a number of poor law unions set up separate wards for the 'insane'. Once the lunacy commissioners were empowered to inspect after 1845, they tended to inspect the wards for the insane rather more frequently than those for 'idiots'.

---

5   Idem.
6   Idem. For Foucault, see p. 79.
7   Borsay (2005), pp. 27–28.

Thus if Adam, within the terminology of the day, had been classified as an 'idiot' the inspection regime over the provision for him would have been less than strict. If he had been classified as a lunatic, the provision for him would have been made at the cheapest possible level within the workhouse rather than the asylum. Should he have found his way to an asylum, the provision was variable in quality. In the late 1830s the asylum which had been set up near Hereford in 1799 was investigated by a select committee:

> Patients were overcrowded, restraint was widely practiced and cold baths were used as a therapy but also as a punishment. The visitors reported to local justices that the asylum 'was not in that State, either as relates to ventilation, to classification, to employment, to moral treatment, to recreation, and religious conversation to convalescents, which they would wish to prevail'.

The county magistrates refused a licence, but one was issued by the JPs of the city of Hereford, allowing this asylum to stay open until 1853.[8] Within the world of the asylums, there was the specialization of the 'idiot' asylums. In 1848, the National Asylum for Idiots – Earlswood – opened its doors at temporary premises in North London. Within these asylums classes catered for a range of abilities. Adam would have found himself 'at the lower levels', where:

> the emphasis fell on basic life skills like feeding, dressing and speech. Teaching methods were sometimes ingenious. Numbers were put to music. Letters were demonstrated with wooden aids. And clothing was even proposed to 'form a series of graduated exercises in buttoning and unbuttoning, tying and untying, lacing and unlacing, buckling and unbuckling, fastening and unfastening with hooks and eyes'.[9]

Borsay traces the way in which thinking about those with cognitive deficits developed during the Victorian period, and the consequent institutional changes. This included the addition of the term 'feeble minded' to the armoury of descriptive terms. In 1866, P. Martin Duncan and William Millard published *A Manual for the Classification,*

---

8   Ibid., pp. 72–73.
9   Ibid., p. 99. Children in the 'top class' were expected to be able to read biblical passages 'with tolerable correctness'.

Training and Education of the Feeble Minded, Imbecile and Idiotic.[10] The category of feeble-mindedness opened the door once more to the medicalization of disability. In 1908, Alfred Tredgold's *Textbook of Mental Deficiency* insisted that feeble-mindedness was 'not the lowest grade of the normal but a...definite abnormality – that it... [was], in fact, a disease'.[11] Equally, it created a pressure for the development of the category of 'special' education. The 1889 Royal Commission recommended schooling for the 'blind, deaf and dumb, and the educable class of imbeciles' to prevent them from becoming not only 'a burden to themselves but a weighty burden to the State'.[12]

Tredgold's book on mental deficiency was, as Borsay points out, still being reissued after the end of the Second World War. It is at that time, but in another country, that perhaps the darkest episode in the history of disability took place. The events are recorded in the second volume of Ian Kershaw's monumental biography of Adolf Hitler. Between February and May 1939, Hans Hefelman, an official in the Fuehrer Chancellery, acting on the instructions of Karl Brandt, Hitler's doctor, conducted the consultations with sympathetic doctors which led to the setting up of the 'Reich Committee for the Scientific Registration of Serious Hereditary and Congenital Suffering'. It is estimated that under the aegis of this committee between 5000 and 8000 children were put to death, mostly by injections with the barbiturate luminal. In July of the same year, Hitler expressed his view to Hans Heinrich Lammers (Head of the Reich Chancellery), Martin Bormann (at that stage Rudolph Hess's secretary), and Dr. Leonardo Conti (newly appointed Reich Health Leader and State Secretary for Health in the Reich Ministry of the Interior) that 'he favoured mercy killing for seriously ill mental patients. Better use of hospitals, doctors and nursing staff could be made in war, he stated'. As a result of these comments, Conti was commissioned to study the feasibility of such a programme. Viktor Brack, assistant to the head of the Fuehrer Chancellery, Philipp Bouhler, and Hefelman's superior, fearing the loss of the initiative to Conti, and to the Ministry of the Interior, had Hefelman draw up a short statistical memorandum on the asylums,

---

10   Ibid., p. 102.
11   Ibid., p. 103.
12   Ibid., p. 106.

and presented it to Bouhler. A subsequent meeting of doctors in the Reich Chancellery suggested that around 60,000 patients might be eligible, and an organization was set up under Brack's direction at Tiergarttenstraße 4, in Berlin Charlottenberg. It was from this address that the subsequent euthanasia action took its name: *Aktion T-4*. The following October, Hitler had a single sentence typed on his headed notepaper, which he signed and backdated to 1 September, the day on which the war had broken out: 'Reichsleiter Bouhler and Dr. med. Brandt are commissioned with the responsibility of extending the authority of specified doctors so that, after critical assessment of their condition, those adjudged incurably ill can be granted mercy death.' It was the medical staff of the asylums themselves who were asked to select the patients for mercy killing; the killings were mostly by carbon monoxide gas in selected asylums, of which the most notorious were Grafeneck, Hadamar, Bernberg, Brandenburg, Hartheim and Sonnenstein.[13]

Within the United Kingdom, within living memory, the treatment of those with learning disabilities and/or mental health problems, although in no way reaching the supreme cruelty of the Nazi regime, has not brought credit to our society. Many of the elements of our Victorian heritage persisted, and were the occasional source of scandal. Nicholas Timmins records in his history of the welfare State, *The Five Giants*, that when Dick Crossman arrived at the Department of Health and Social Security in 1969, one of his first duties was to deal with Geoffrey Howe's 83,000-word report on the cruelty and cover up at the long stay Ely Hospital in Cardiff. As *The Times* editorial had it at the time: 'After these distressing revelations and the helpful recommendations of the committee of enquiry, it should not be too difficult to get Ely Hospital up to a reasonable standard. But people will want to know how far the rot had spread through similar institutions.'[14] Against departmental resistance, Crossman had the report published in full and insisted that a hospital advisory service be set up to visit long stay institutions. Timmins records that what followed was a 'decade long catalogue of further horrors and enquiries' on the long stay wards of Farleigh, Whittingham, Napsbury, South Ockenden, St. Augustine's

---

13   Summarized from Kershaw (2000), pp. 258–261.
14   28 March 1969, editorial.

and Normansfield. Tam Dalyell was Parliamentary Private Secretary to Crossman, and chronicled his reactions during a ministerial visit to Frien Barnet:

> I never saw Crossman so subdued or shaken by the stench and the soaking walls and the consequent treatment of the helpless, incontinent and usually relationless patients. [...] In his car on the way back to the Elephant and Castle, he repeated: 'I am responsible for the worst kind of Dickensian, Victorian loony bin.'[15]

In the same year as the Ely report there was an adjournment debate in the House of Commons on the problem of autism. The number of children with autism was increasing, though there was a lack of appropriate diagnostic facilities. Dennis Howell, then under-secretary at the Department of Education and Science, indicated that the department intended 'to give more thought to autistic children'. During the debate, a survey was mentioned of 42 'autistics' who were aged over 17. Half of them were in mental hospitals.[16]

The editor of *The Times* believed that 'some of Ely's troubles came from overcrowding, which came from lack of development of the alternative for long stay hospital patients of this type, namely community care'. Over the decades, the movement from institutional to community care which was initiated by Powell's water tower speech[17] proceeded at a snail's pace. It was only in 1986 that the first of the long stay hospitals was closed. The process was not only slow, it was ineffective. In December 1986, the audit commission produced a hard hitting report on the introduction of community care:

> Much of the £6 billion a year that services for the elderly, mentally ill, and handicapped cost was being misspent... The finance, organization and staffing of the transfer from NHS to community care was such that it was 'little short of amazing' that any successful schemes had been introduced.[18]

---

15   Timmins (1996), pp. 258–259.
16   London *Times* 'Tackling the problem of autism', 24 May 1969, referring to the adjournment debate on the previous day.
17   See p. 115.
18   Timmins (1996), p. 417.

As we review this historical material, some very contemporary issues come to the surface: how to give quality assurance to the care of those with cognitive deficits, especially when social and political pressure was for the most economic solutions to 'problems'; the consequent urge to classify and the associated delimitation of disability within medical and/educational terms; the failure of the capitalist economy in its high Victorian noon to see people with disabilities in general as nothing other than non-economically productive members of society to be reinserted – wherever possible – within capitalist systems. Michel Foucault suggests that in writing history, we are writing the history of the present. So let us turn to the present, and see the changing situation in which Adam has found himself since diagnosis.

We can best describe that situation by seeing that Adam is caught within a hierarchy of control. That hierarchy begins in his immediate environment, be it the family home or, as later in his life, the residential school. Beyond that are the local authorities for health, education and social care which provide his funding. Those local authorities have a complicated relationship with the Welsh Assembly, which in turn has a similarly complicated relationship with the Westminster Government. Beyond all of these is the influence of the European Community, as well as the institutions belonging to the wider diplomatic community. At any of these levels, events can occur which impact upon the space within which Adam is controlled.

In 2001, in the foreword to the White Paper, *Valuing People,* Tony Blair talked about 'improving the life chances for people with learning disabilities'.[19] In Adam's life, his life chances have indeed been improved in a number of ways. There have been improvements in the administration of special needs education, though the system is widely recognized as being far from perfect, and, while noting the Scottish provision for mediation, it is inherently conflictual.[20] Improvements have also taken place in the regulation of social care.[21] There has been increasing pressure for different government agencies and services

---

19   Department of Health (2001).
20   See the Education (Additional Support for Learning) (Scotland) Act of 2004.
21   For example in the Care Standards Act of 2000 and the Health and Social Care (Community Health and Standards) Act of 2003.

to work in more effective collaboration with each other.[22] There is a greater strategic focus at different levels of government, a preparedness to take an *overview* rather than leaving everything to the vagaries of local decision making.[23] Adam and ourselves as his carers have been the beneficiaries in the enhancement of our human rights, and have much greater legislative protection from discrimination.[24] There are better structures for representing the views and interests of those who do not have the capacity to do this for themselves.[25] There is a higher level of awareness of autism, and preparedness to fund research into the main unanswered scientific questions.[26] Yet for all this, the system by which Adam is cared for and controlled still contains chronic failings. I will now seek to show how that charge can be sustained in the areas of health, education and social services.

While this book was being written, *Healthcare for All*, the Independent Inquiry into Access to Healthcare for People with Learning Disabilities, led by Sir Jonathan Michael, produced its report. This report had been commissioned at the invitation of Patricia Hewitt (Secretary of State for Health until 2007) in response to an original report by Mencap *Death by Indifference* which was made up of six case studies of people with learning disabilities who had died while in NHS care. The Michael report is hard hitting: although it heard of examples of good practice, 'witnesses described some appalling examples of discrimination, abuse and neglect across the range of health

---

22   For example in Section 75 of the National Health Service Act of 2006, with similar provision for Wales in section 33 of the National Health Service (Wales) Act of the same year.

23   In April 2008, the deputy minister for social services, Gwenda Thomas, launched the Autistic Spectrum Disorder Strategic Action Plan for Wales. The Westminster Government announced in February 2009 that they would introduce regulations and statutory guidance to ensure local authorities and all other local agencies include children with autism in their plans for children's services.

24   Importantly the Human Rights Act of 1998, the Disability Rights Commission Act of 1999 and the new Disability Discrimination Act of 2005.

25   The Mental Capacity Act of 2005 has been controversial, but no-one could doubt the importance of the issues being addressed.

26   In October 2007, the Welsh Assembly Government announced funding for the establishment of a chair of Autistic Spectrum Disorder at the Department of Psychology in Cardiff. As of the beginning of 2009, the Medical Research Council was funding 11 research projects concerned with autism, to the value of about £1.5 million per annum. http://www.mrc.ac.uk/Ourresearch/ResearchFocus/Autism/index.htm [accessed 22 February 2009].

services'.[27] Michael speaks of 'negative attitudes and values towards people with learning disabilities', of 'a failure to deliver equal treatment, or to treat people with dignity or respect'.[28] These and the quotations which follow are largely taken from the Executive Summary, although the whole report repays careful attention. As Michael points out, the existence of a learning disability can stop people getting treatment for a non-related health issue: 'People with learning disabilities find it much harder than other people to access assessment and treatment for general health problems that have nothing directly to do with their disability.'[29] Specifically relevant to Adam's situation is a comment in the body of the report: 'Together, the evidence suggests there is unmet health need amongst people with learning disabilities. Research in Wales supports the suggestion that levels of unmet need are, furthermore, relatively high.'[30] If this is the case, then it is not surprising that the health care which is received in respect of the learning disability can fall short of the mark. Michael specifies a number of areas of concern:

- Lack of attention to the expertise of parents and carers. They 'often find their opinions and assessments ignored by healthcare professionals, even though they often have the best information about, and understanding of, the people they support. They struggle to be accepted as effective partners in care by those involved in providing general healthcare; their complaints are not heard; they are expected to do too much of the care that should be provided by the health system and are often required to provide care beyond their personal resources.'[31]

- Lack of staff expertise, particularly amongst 'those working in general health care': 'The health needs, communication problems, and cognitive impairment characteristic of learning disability in particular are poorly understood. Staff are not

---

27   Michael (2008), p. 7.
28   Ibid., p. 8.
29   Ibid., p. 7.
30   Ibid., p. 16, referring to work in 2002 by the Welsh Centre for Learning Disabilities.
31   Ibid., p. 7.

familiar with what help they should provide or from whom to get expert advice.'[32] This lack of staff expertise would naturally hinder the development of good working relationships with parents and carers, as staff would be unable to be confident in their own knowledge, and, coming to our next point, would equally hinder intra-organizational partnership work. Michael specifies that 'lack of awareness of the health needs of people with learning disabilities is striking in primary care',[33] that is in general practice, at first point of consultation. The training and education provided 'to undergraduates and post-graduate clinical staff' as well as post qualification training is very limited.[34]

- Organizational failures, especially in developing partnership working: 'Partnership working and communication (between different agencies providing care, between services for different age groups, and across NHS primary, secondary and tertiary boundaries) is poor in relation to services for adults with learning disabilities.'[35]

- Failures in the collection of information: 'People with learning disabilities are not visible or identifiable to health services, and hence the quality of their care is impossible to assess. Data and information on this subset of the population and their journeys through the general healthcare system is largely lacking and what exists is inadequately co-coordinated or understood.'[36] Often people with learning disabilities are presented with pleas of lack of resources to meet need. As we have seen, the role of lack of resources can be an important legal issue. This is in the context of a data-poor system, which has no means of assessing the effectiveness of the use of resources in this particular area of concern.

32   Ibid., p. 7.
33   Ibid., p. 8.
34   Ibid., p. 8.
35   Ibid., p. 7.
36   Ibid., p. 8.

- Problems of regulation and prioritization: 'neither healthcare inspectors nor regulators focus specifically on the quality of health services provided for people with learning disability, so they slip through the inspectorial and regulatory net'.[37] In the NHS operational plans for 2008–9 to 2010–11, the whole area of learning disabilities is placed at Tier 3 Local Action rather than Tier 1 National Requirement or Tier 2 National Priority for Local Delivery. At this level the Department of Health 'would not expect to be involved in performance management'.[38]

I will now turn from health to social care. The organizational relationship between health and social care is strange, and arises from the different historical circumstances in which these services developed. At central level, within the Department of Health, they come under the same ministerial supervision. Within the Department, at the time of writing there is a Parliamentary Under Secretary of State for Health and a Parliamentary Under Secretary of State for Social Care. However, at a local level the provision of social care is in the hands of local authorities, while the provision of health care arises from the separate structures – and legislative framework – of the National Health Service. It is the Commission for Social Care Inspection (CSCI) which has the responsibility for maintaining standards, within English social care settings. It is worth noting that the inspection of care services for children was transferred from CSCI to Ofsted in 2007, and that thus much of the information recently produced by CSCI tends to be slanted towards adult services. In January 2008, the Commission produced its report *The State of Social Care in England*. From this report, I am going to take a range of aspects of the work of social care which impact directly upon the lives of those, and seek to identify weaknesses in parallel to the information on health care which I have already put forward from the Michael report. The Commission acknowledges an increasing level of rationing in social care, to which it had alluded in

---

37 Ibid., p. 8.
38 http://www.dh.gov.uk/en/Publicationsandstatistics/Publications/
    PublicationsPolicyAndGuidance/DH_082542 [accessed 29 July 2008]. The
    information regarding the system of tiers is referred to by Michael, and given in the
    original document on pp. 5–6.

a previous report: 'The state of social care 2005–06 drew attention to the "ever-rising eligibility criteria for access to services" and raised concerns about the impact on people of targeting social care resources so narrowly.'[39] One of the reasons given for this increased rationing of social care has been the impact upon social care systems of people like Adam as they grow to early adulthood:

> *Younger people with complex needs.* The high cost of meeting the needs of younger adults with very complex needs, with knock-on effects for other groups, was a recurrent theme across the six sites. [In depth field work was conducted in six anonymised English councils] In particular, high cost (and typically out-of-area) support for small numbers of people with learning disabilities was often cited as the explanation for budgetary deficits. Support for these people would be prioritized but with consequences for people with less complex needs.[40]

The idea that the Adam's needs may well be prioritized, over, say, domiciliary services in the care of the elderly does not mean to say that the financial burden which he and others represent is willingly accepted by local authorities, because of the pressure which they put upon the overall system. Financial scarcity is also having a major impact upon social work practice:

> Many managers and practitioners believed that social workers were becoming de-skilled and that the demands of budgetary control and performance targets were undermining capacity for reflective practice and a person-centred response. For example, they said: 'Long-standing social workers are questioning why they are still in the profession. The traditional approach of sitting down with somebody for a couple of hours, going over their problems and helping them to fill in forms doesn't exist any longer. It's all financial assessments, inputting information onto the computer and performing against targets.'[41]

The Commission identifies a culture which will describe people in terms of their eligible needs, rather than seeing the whole of a needful person. It is one aspect of that labelling which is so familiar to

---

39   Commission for Social Care Inspection (2008), p. 127.
40   Ibid., p. 129.
41   Ibid., p. 135.

disabled people and their carers: 'You can pick up an assessment and you are so clearly reading something written by somebody who is driven by eligible needs and trying to find out what these are – not trying to find out the person.'[42] One of the particular ways in which professionals will cope with the tension between resources and need is by signposting, indicating the availability of other resources in the private or voluntary sectors: 'The nature and quality of signposting appeared to depend upon the skills and personal commitment of individual workers – some did no more than provide lists of addresses and telephone numbers; others attempted to support individuals in making contact and arranging appropriate services.'[43]

Given the relationship of financial and institutional ethos, and the way in which institutional ethos impacts upon the lives of those with learning disabilities, it is well here to record some actual figures. These are taken from the Executive Summary to *The State of Social Care in England*: 'Over 2 million people of all ages, including children, and from every community, used social care services arranged by local councils during 2006–07. Councils spent £14.2 billion on social care for all adults.'[44] The spend on social care for adults in 2005–6 had increased by 4.5 per cent in real terms since 2004–5. Of this spending, 21 per cent was on adults aged 18 to 64 with learning disabilities. By 2005–6 there was a 14 per cent increase in spending on adults with learning disabilities and physical and sensory impairments since 2003–4.[45] In the Comprehensive Spending Review for 2007, the government announced the intention of 'an increase in Department of Health direct funding for adult social care of £190 million by 2010–11'.[46] The figures look large and generous, and are certainly increasing, but the reason that they are increasing is exactly in response to the financial pressures upon the social care system.

Early in the life of the current UK Parliament, the Select Committee on Education and Skills gave particular attention to the difficulties surrounding the education of those with special educational needs.

---

42   Ibid., p. 135.
43   Ibid., p. 137.
44   CSCI (2008), Executive Summary, p. 3.
45   Ibid., p. 6.
46   Ibid., p. 4.

Their First Report in February 2007 summarized the depressing conclusions of their Third Report of the session 2005–2006. There had been no such report undertaken during the life of the previous Parliament, and

> our report identified serious flaws in the SEN system with regards to consistency of provision, the statementing process and teacher training. It called for a statutory requirement for local authorities to provide a broad range of support for youngsters with SEN – including the provision of Special Schools – and recommended a set of minimum standards so that parents would no longer have to 'fight' to achieve a better outcome for their child.[47]

To this report, 'the Government response…was very disappointing'. The committee's disappointment was that

> on a number of significant issues [the Government] did not accurately portray recommendations that we made, and the Government's failure to even consider changing the current statementing process was a real missed opportunity. *As we said at the time, despite clear evidence that the process is not working as it should, the Government relied on the argument that 'no-one has a better alternative'. This is not acceptable. If the system is not working properly it is the Government's duty to look for a better way forward.*[48]

The crucial statement here is that 'the system is not working properly' – it is a theme to which we have recurred on a number of occasions throughout this book, that dysfunctional systems affect the lives of individuals in chronic ways.

If the state of health care, social care, and education for those with learning disabilities is as I have described them, then something should be done. It should not be accepted that there is no alternative. We live within a system that so often takes people with disabilities as somehow impaired in their humanity. That kind of talk can actually be distracting attention from the real impairments in the system for their care, which is not well, which is broken. Often this struggle comes down to micro-politics, to the unending battle of individual

---

47   http://www.publications.parliament.uk/pa/cm200607/cmselect/
       cmeduski/301/30104.htm#note1 [accessed 14 January 2009], paragraph 9.
48   Ibid., para. 10 – the text in italics is highlighted in the original report.

carers to make the system work for those for whom they care. I have already described that struggle, and would like to go now beyond that to the ways in which we can address problems with structures.

The immediate difficulty is the lack of public awareness that there is a difficulty. An indication is given by two quotations from *The State of Social Care*: 'Social services always seemed to be one of those services that consumed copious amounts of money and had an overspend every year. We had to ensure that it didn't keep consuming more and more council tax' and 'When members are setting their priorities they will speak to people on the streets and ask them what is important to them. Social care won't feature in that.'[49] There is, at all levels of government, a priority towards the keeping down of taxes. This combines with a public indifference to some aspects of the care of those with learning disabilities. If the question is asked explicitly, most people would say, whatever their personal acquaintance with the issue, that those with learning disabilities should receive high quality care. If asked separately whether local and national taxes should be kept as low as possible the answer would often be 'yes'. For the majority, the priority towards lower spending is based on a rational calculation that the issues relating to public service provision will not affect them. Those who have no need of public services like to think that they will not need them; they psychologically block out that possibility. People with learning disabilities have a classic problem of the minority within a democratic system in which the people as a whole by democratic vote decide through their Parliamentary representatives on the level of public spending. The majority in considering their democratic options will meet the needs of the majority rather than of the minority. However, this minority need high levels of public spending in order to maintain their personal equality within the democratic system.

Let us however assume for a moment that there are high levels of awareness regarding learning disability, combined with a public willingness to do all things necessary to support those with learning disabilities, including those with autism. There would then be an expectation of political and legislative action on behalf of those with learning disabilities. Yet, even in the system as it stands at present, there is a considerable mismatch between legislative intention and

---

49   CSCI (2008), p. 130.

actual change. We can find a specific example of a broader problem by going back to the pages of the Michael review:

> The Government through the Department of Health, the Department for Children, Schools and Families and the Department for Innovation, Universities and Skills (formerly DfES) and the Department for Communities and Local Government have taken steps to ensure that there is a comprehensive legislative and advisory framework to prevent discrimination [against those with learning disabilities]. However, the evidence suggests that there is a lack of awareness and understanding in the wider NHS concerning the action that this legislation and guidance should prompt and hence, *behaviour is slow to change*.

The broader problem which needs to be addressed is that even where a comprehensive legislative and advisory framework is in place 'behaviour is slow to change'.[50] Thus, political action in itself, under the current constitutional dispensation, does not provide an exhaustive and indeed expeditious solution of the injustices faced by people with learning disabilities. Adam experiences a gap between language and the daily reality around him; they do not meet. In the same way, there is a gap between the language of statute, guidance and regulation on one hand, and everyday experience on the other.

The question which thus appears is how we should think and act in order to bring about change. If there is an injustice, how do we right it? Essential to this is the development within the last decade of thinking about human rights, and their incorporation into statute law. Within a democratic system, human rights protect the standing of minorities and of the voiceless. In his magisterial *Civil Liberties and Human Rights in England and Wales,* David Feldman 'in order to clarify some basic issues' examines in the first chapter – entitled 'Some basic values: civil liberties, human rights and autonomy' – 'the philosophical background to civil liberties and rights, and the relationship between models of rights, models of democracy, and constitutional structures, in order to explain the position from which the discussion of concrete rights and liberties proceeds in the rest of the book'. The output is 'concrete rights and liberties'. It is only those which protect, in their weakness, people on the autistic spectrum and their carers.

---

50   Michael (2008), p. 8.

Those concrete rights emerge from the 'philosophical background'; it is that philosophical background which I would seek now to hold in question, from the perspective of Adam himself. It is not surprising to find that Feldman, in common with others, predicates his discussion upon shared humanity. In a section in which he is responding to the question '...is liberty generally, or a particular liberty, a good in itself, or does it derive its value from its capacity to advance ulterior goods?' he states that: 'Any idea of liberty must necessarily depend ultimately on an evaluation of the proper ends of human beings in the light of a vision of the human condition.'[51] The question of liberty generates the question of purpose: what projects can human beings appropriately contemplate either individually or collectively; what can they – and what should they – use their liberty for. We have seen earlier a number of aspects of Adam as he is. He does not live – in the same way – in the successive chronological time that is the experience of others. Nor does he generally form large purposes. His purposive behaviour is restricted to the range of his autistic obsessions, which close out other purposes. For Adam, the question to be asked is not of proper ends, but of not having ends and purposes. It may be suggested here that in its first principles the law here does not recognize him. This becomes clear in the second question which Feldman asks: 'do liberties and rights derive their worth from their value to individuals only, or does it depend also on their value to society?' We have already seen the ways in which Adam does not recognize the social, and as a consequence, he experiences his own individuality, and other people experience his individuality, otherwise. Sociability and individuality are not essential to his being. Again, for Feldman it goes back to a vision of what humanity is: 'The belief in human beings as social individuals, beings for whom both sociability and individuality are essential parts of their make up, is ultimately a deontological belief.' This belongs to a different world to the one which I inhabit. In that world, I believe that many, but not all, human beings are – to a greater or lesser extent – social individuals. Unless my belief in this area was to include all, I could not give it the deontological, compulsive force which Feldman allows it to exercise upon the whole of the legal system. Here, we need to retrace our steps a little, and to be very clear within what language

---

51   Feldman (2002), p. 6.

game Feldman is setting the term 'human rights'. 'It is,' says Feldman, 'here used in technical sense. It would be possible to use it to refer to rights which people have merely by being part of a human society. It would then be necessary to consider what rights, if any, people have intrinsically as human beings. To avoid the need for this, human rights will be treated as a legal term of art, referring to those rights which have been enshrined in international human rights treaties, particularly in the period since the end of World War II.' Feldman has rightly made a distinction between civil liberties – 'essentially rights not to be interfered with, or "negative rights" as they are sometimes called' – whereas 'positive rights' are 'people's claims upon the State for help'. The bridge between these two related realms would seem to the the term 'humanity' itself. Yet when he is looking at human rights as such, it would seem that Feldman takes them in a very restricted sense. 'Human rights' becomes a legal term of art, specifically referring to what has been enacted in human rights treaties especially since the end of the Second World War. This then takes us to what might be called 'legislative intention'. It would not have been in the thought of those who framed such treaties, until at least more recent times, to consider within their sense of common humanity those with disabilities. Insofar that an awareness of disability rights has gradually increased, it was still yet not in the thought of the framers of international treaties to include within their sense of common humanity those with autism. They would especially not have been aware of the specific challenges which autism presents to our sense of common humanity. I do not believe that such treaties have exhaustively defined our humanity; I do not any more than that believe that the text of such legal enactments exhaustively defines the rights of humanity.

At this point we turn our attention to some of the actual international enactments which are relevant to Adam's life. On 20 December 1971, United Nations General Assembly resolution 2856 made the Declaration on the Rights of Mentally Retarded Persons. The document affirms a belief that the rights of 'mentally retarded persons' arise from general human rights: 'Reaffirming faith in human rights and fundamental freedoms and in the principles of peace, of the dignity and worth of the human person and of social justice proclaimed in the Charter...' However, beyond this, the rights of those with learning disabilities and others are hedged around with qualification. The ideal is normalization. The document does not tread successfully the line between inclusion and normalization, and might be considered to be treating the disabled as the actually or potentially able: 'Bearing in mind the necessity of assisting mentally retarded persons to develop their abilities in various fields of activities and of promoting their integration as far as possible in normal life...' Clause 2 of the Declaration establishes the right to 'such education, training, rehabilitation and guidance as will enable him [sic] to develop his ability and maximum potential'. It is a conservative document in its views on the relationship of social care and the economy, and in particular the capacity of different national economies to sustain the lives of people with disabilities. All those who have been engaged with social care in the United Kingdom are aware of the post-code lottery. It is of little comfort to realize that in 1971, as now, the post-code lottery is a global phenomenon. The General Assembly 'proclaims this Declaration on the Rights of Mentally Retarded Persons' but is 'aware that certain countries, at their present stage of development, can devote only limited efforts to this end'. The key problem occurs in Clause 1 of the Declaration: 'The mentally retarded person has, to the maximum degree of feasibility, the same rights as other human beings.' This is to allow a disability (or disabilities) in and of themselves to impinge upon the human rights of the person who is disabled, and thus, by implication, to throw into doubt the recognition of the full humanity of a person with disabilities. The full implications of this are made explicit in Clause 7, which is the last clause and which frankly acknowledges that rights may be restricted or denied.

> Whenever mentally retarded persons are unable, because of the severity of their handicap, to exercise all their rights in a meaningful way or it should become necessary to restrict or deny some or all of these rights, the procedure used for that restriction or denial of rights must contain proper legal safeguards against every form of abuse. This procedure must be based on an evaluation of the social capability of the mentally retarded person by qualified experts and must be subject to periodic review and to the right of appeal to higher authorities.

In this clause we see a the weaving together of a number of themes which have appeared elsewhere in this book: the concept of 'severity' being used to justify the differential treatment of those with disabilities, so that the severely disabled become the excluded other of the 'community' of those with disabilities; the concept of 'severity' being in turn predicated on 'social capability', which exposes the lives of those at one end of the autistic spectrum to specific dangers; the elevation of the 'able', of 'qualified experts', of 'higher authorities' as those who delimit the extent of the rights which the disabled will enjoy. The document took as its starting place the rights which those with disabilities should enjoy, by dint of their humanity, but concluded by setting limits to those rights in extreme cases. The starting point should have been the whole of humanity including the extremes of humanity.

On 3 May 2008, the Convention on the Rights of Persons with Disabilities and its Optional Protocol entered into force following the 20th ratification by a member-State of the United Nations the previous month. This Convention does not strictly apply to Adam's day-to-day life, as the United Kingdom, while signing the original convention in February 2008, has itself yet to ratify. Nor has the United Kingdom ratified the *Optional Protocol*, which provides a robust mechanism for the enforcement of the rights contained in the convention, as the introductory words of the *Protocol* suggest:

> 1.1 A State Party to the present Protocol ('State Party') recognizes the competence of the Committee on the Rights of Persons with Disabilities ('the Committee') to receive and consider communications from or on behalf of individuals or groups of individuals subject to its jurisdiction who claim to be victims of a violation by that State Party of the provisions of the Convention.[52]

For all kinds of other reasons, the capacity of the United Nations to enforce its collective will on states party is a matter of public discussion. Once again, we come across a collective body which, while wanting to give the appearance of capacity and power, knows its own existence to be marked by incapacity, by impairment. To call the United Nations

---

52   http://www2.ohchr.org/english/law/disabilities-op.htm [accessed 6 May 2008].

a disabled body is in no sense to sit in judgement upon it. Article 3 of the Convention sets out its general principles:

> The principles of the present Convention shall be: respect for inherent dignity, individual autonomy including the freedom to make one's own choices, and independence of persons; non-discrimination; full and effective participation and inclusion in society; respect for difference and acceptance of persons with disabilities as part of human diversity and humanity; equality of opportunity; accessibility; equality between men and women; respect for the evolving capacities of children with disabilities and respect for the right of children with disabilities to preserve their identities.

In general, these principles are commendable goals for the flourishing of people with disabilities. However, here, as so often, we see the nature of autism presenting challenges to the very frameworks within which it is captured. In what way can Adam be given the freedom to make his own choices? In what sense can he ever be 'independent', in any meaningful sense of the term? As his difficulty with socialization is an inherent part of his disability, in what way can 'full and effective' participation be a desirable intention? If Adam is to be given equality of opportunity as against a non-autistic person, in exactly what will that equality of opportunity consist? If a person with autism is meant to be provided with access, are we (neurotypicals) willing to make the adaptations to our day-to-day environment which would make it constantly accessible to Adam? If children with disabilities are intended to 'preserve their identities', how can this be applied to somebody whose different sense of 'identity' is at the heart of his disability?

The appeal to human rights is at the heart of the remedy for the injustices which a voiceless minority will suffer within a democratic society. However, the rhetoric of human rights will not take us all the way to the remedy which is needed. It fails on three accounts: that it is framed without in advance including people with autism within its definition of the human. As a result, when, by making use of the talk of human rights, desirable outcomes are formulated, they are not in keeping with the nature of severe autism, or any disability which poses such a direct challenge to what we think of as the givens of human existence. Third and finally, the enforceability of rights, while being a protection against the power of the majority within the democratic State, is fatally dependent upon the willingness of the State to accede to the enforcement of those rights. Sandra Fredman in her book *Human Rights Transformed – positive rights and positive duties* discusses the ways in which socio-economic rights are hedged around with limitations, and that rights have been conceived as limits on the power of the State, rather than constraining the way in which that power is exercised.[53] The solution to this is not to retreat from talk of human rights, but rather to reformulate the doctrine of human rights in a more extreme form, to think of hyper-rights. As a theologian, I would want to argue that Christian thinking provides an advanced vindication for such 'hyper-rights', and that the Church has a special role of advocacy in the vindication of those rights. The doctrine of the Incarnation suggests that in Christ Jesus, God became fully human. Than this, there could be no greater vindication imagined for human rights. It is at this point that we also see the importance of the biblical material which shows the development of Jesus' thinking about disability, and the talk about the disabled God. If our talk about human rights is predicated upon the Christ of the cross, our sense of humanity includes in advance those who are disabled. We are thus led to a political theology, which is asked to reflect upon the political circumstances of the disabled as it has already been described in this chapter.

Within Christian thought, there is a spectrum of ways of considering the relationship of faith and politics. At one end of this spectrum is a tradition of apartness relative to the State, and indeed of a kind of hostility to the public sphere. Tertullian tells us in *The Apology*: 'But as those in whom all ardour in the pursuit of glory and honour is dead, we have no pressing inducement to take part in your public meetings; nor is there anything more entirely foreign to us than affairs of State. We acknowledge one all-embracing commonwealth – the world.'[54] At the other end of the spectrum are the insights of liberation theology. In his preface to Gustavo Gutiérrez's *A Theology of Liberation*, first published in Spanish in 1971, Professor Christopher Rowland gives an account of a lecture by Gutiérrez during his year at Cambridge as visiting professor of Latin American studies in the late 1980s, and asks the question 'What is liberation theology?' It is:

---

53   Fredman (2008), p. 30 in section E, Conclusion.
54   *Apology*, 38.

nothing if it is not a way of being with the vulnerable, of accompanying the suffering Christ in the contemporary world. It is a means of intellectual and ethical reorientation which offers an understanding of God from within a commitment to the poor and marginalized and a means of thinking afresh about reality or the ways in which we articulate it to one another. We are being summoned to embark upon a process of wrestling with the reality of the wider world of injustice and suffering of the majority of people and discover God.[55]

Without excluding other possibilities in the relationship between faith and politics, it is in this part of the spectrum that I would locate myself. This affiliation existed before Adam's diagnosis and subsequent events, but was affirmed through those experiences. In the first place, while not believing that salvation is won by good works, it was necessary to act. Tertullian identified the chief motivators of political engagement as 'the pursuit of glory and honour', but his turning away from the political and erecting a substantial barrier between the sacred world of the church and the secular world of the political was simply not an option for me, there was a 'pressing inducement' to take part in the public sphere, in a situation which had nothing of 'glory and honour' about it. As it was necessary to act, so it was necessary to have a theology of action. Rowlands in his preface cites some words of the seventeenth-century English radical Gerrard Winstanley, which, had I been aware of them at the time, would have had a poignant force: 'words and writings were all nothing, and must die, for action is the life of all, and if thou dost not act, thou dost nothing.' Liberation theology offered a way of 'being with the vulnerable'; it taught me how to do this. This book is about the profound ethical and intellectual orientation that such a being with the vulnerable wrought: liberation theology provided a commentary upon, and an explanation of what was actually happening. Liberation theology arose from reflection upon the needs of the poor in Latin America, from the 1960s onwards. Its applicability is to all those who neediness is absolute, and thence to Adam and others with profound learning disability. Martin Lloyd Williams speaks of parents and carers who are struggling for decent access to education, social care and other support, including

---

55   Gutiérrez (2001), p. xii.

respite care: 'Such parents have no desire to act in militant ways but their experience does provide a point of contact with Jesus who was also not received.'[56] In the face of such injustice, there is actually no choice but to act in a militant way, to be radicalized, to ask what true liberation would be.

I believe that the answer to that question comes specifically in reflection upon the thinking of the first generation of Christians, to which thinking the letters of St. Paul so much belong. I am aware that by the choice of those documents, I am turning to sources which have very much underwritten contemporary Evangelical faith and practice within the Church. I am wanting to argue that their true importance belongs outside the sphere of the sacred, and takes us in a different direction to the classic Evangelical interpretation of them. The way to approach these documents is to ask what problems Paul and the early Christians to whom he provided leadership were responding. One might suggest that among those problems two were of the highest significance. First, the question was to what extent the Christ event had changed the relationship of his first followers to the Jewish law. If the gracefulness of that event was sufficient, was there any need to keep to every provision of the *Torah*? Insofar as the *Torah* was no longer determinative, which, exactly, of its provisions should be observed? Second, the Christ event had led the first Christians to conclude that they were living in the end time. A trace of a key element of their faith is preserved in the creedal affirmation: 'He will come again in glory to judge both the living and the dead.' The first Christians assumed that, as they were living in the end time, this second coming of the Messiah would be an imminent event. Their puzzlement is that of millenarian groups down the centuries: if we believe that an apocalyptic event is about to happen, why has it not yet happened? They lived in a state of indefinite postponement, as the Christian Church has done ever since.

We can now transfer this thinking to our thinking about the political situation of disabled people and their carers. Early in this chapter, we reviewed the longer term history of the care of those with learning disabilities, as well as the specific reforming policy and legislation which has appeared within the last decade. The attempt was to show

---

56   Williams (2007), p. 24.

the development of the law relating to those with learning disabilities in all its massivity, and in some of its detail. St. Paul's writings – as well as the wider New Testament witness – allow us to set up a model for our relationship to this legal system. The argument is that although St. Paul's writings are clearly about *Torah*, they are not all about *Torah*: they are a sketch of how Christian thinking can relate to any legal system. Thus, St. Paul affirms the Law, but goes beyond it: 'the whole law is fulfilled in one word, "You shall love your neighbour as yourself."'[57] It is this language of fulfilment that the New Testament relationship to the Law is cast. In the same way, one would wish to affirm – while doing so *critically* – all the developments which have taken place in the decade-long span of legal development which we have considered, but to go beyond that to say that there are things which cannot be contained within the constraints of any legal system, which are love and care themselves. Thus, we would want to prioritize the front line care which Adam receives beyond the legal frameworks and structures within which that care is delivered. That front line care is the fulfilment of those legal frameworks and structures. Furthermore, there is a danger, within those frameworks and structures, that we will live in a state of indefinite postponement. The political situation that we have described has been, certainly since the eighteenth century, one of slow and steady reform, with an accent on slowness. If one were to say that the conditions of life for many people in the 1960s and indeed later were 'Victorian', one would be making precisely this point. By now, this slowness is explicitly self-acknowledged within the political system. In 2005, in his preface to the *Final Report* of the Prime Minister's strategy unit (together with the Department for Work and Pensions, the Department for Education and Skills, and the Office of the Deputy Prime Minister), Tony Blair promised that people with disabilities would 'have full opportunities and choices to improve their quality of life and will be respected and included as equal members of society', and that this would take place by the year 2025. Cynically, one could say that the political system reinforces dependence upon itself by asserting that change can only be achieved in this gradual, incremental way: those who lobby for improvements in the life chances of those with disabilities always need to be coming back for more. If

---

57   Galatians 5:14.

however the necessary changes were to take place, government would, at least in one sense, no longer be necessary. We should have seen all the demands of the law fulfilled.

We need to set all of this in a wider reflection upon the way in which power works, and so to look at the origin and purposes of the State. We are asking the practical and theoretical question of what the State is for, both in theory and in practice, and how the care of those with disabilities fits in with those purposes. In order to do this we can turn once more to Michel Foucault as one of the great twentieth-century theorists of power. For Foucault, power did not simply mean the sovereignty of the State: he believed relationships of power to be at work in all social relations. Before we return to this, let us first look at his thinking about sovereignty. In an important series of lectures delivered at Stanford University in October 1979 – '*Omnes et singulatim*' – *towards a critique of political reason*[58] – Foucault traced the development of the modern nation State. He believed political power to have arisen from pastoral power, contrasting the Greek god with the Shepherd-King of ancient Israel:

> It's not only a matter of saving them all, all together, when danger comes nigh. It's a matter of constant, individualized and final kindness. Constant kindness, for the shepherd ensures his flock's food; every day he attends to their thirst and hunger. The Greek god was asked to provide a fruitful land and abundant crops. He was not asked to foster a flock day by day. And individualized kindness, too, for the shepherd sees that all the sheep, each and every one of them, is fed and saved.[59]

Out of the Jewish tradition was developed Christian thinking about pastoral care, which Foucault suggested to have marked a great point of rupture with the ancient world.

> We can say that Christian pastorate has introduced a game that neither the Greeks nor the Hebrews imagined. A strange game whose elements are life, death, truth, obedience, individuals, self-identity; a game which seems to have nothing to do with the game of the city surviving through the sacrifice of the citizens. Our societies proved to be really demonic since they happened to combine

---

58   Foucault (1988), pp. 57–85.
59   Ibid., p. 62.

those two games – the city-citizen game and the shepherd-flock game – in what we call the modern states.[60]

This sets the simple struggle to access public services in a much wider context. It shows why those who are engaged in that struggle experience the State simultaneously in two different ways, both as extending care to the individual, but also as treating the individual as expendable, one among many in the city. Under the rubric of 'power', Foucault would have regarded State power and pastoral power in the same way. His hostility, his resistance would have been to all forms of power, by whosoever exercised, by priest or king. *Contra Foucault,* I am suggesting that we need to return to the roots of the State in care for those who comprise the State, in care, and nothing besides.

In his thinking about power, we can see worked out one particular example of Foucault's thinking about epistemic breaks. A key commentator on Foucault's work, Lois McNay says this:

> the transition from one episteme to another is conceptualized not as a gradual process but as a sudden and complete rupture. In a matter of a few years the cluster of problems and concepts that preoccupied a preceding era have been entirely abandoned and replaced by a new and incommensurable set of issues.[61]

It was a major part of Foucault's thinking to identify the conditions under which new discourse emerged from old discourse. When I began to write this book, I thought of such an epistemic break, certainly in the areas of discourse which I have been considering, as something which I myself might have experienced or to be a desirable future event; there is now some reason to believe that we are, on a global basis, living through at this moment such a moment of transition. Finally in this chapter, therefore, we will consider our very contemporary predicament.

The new government in 1997 presented itself as marking a decisive break, certainly at very least with the past history of the Labour movement. It had inherited from Labour's past a commitment to public services, to continuing the tradition of the post-war establishment of the welfare State. It also inherited a certain managerialism in the

---

60   Ibid., pp. 70–71.
61   McNay (1994), pp. 64–65.

delivery of those public services: the belief that by central initiative change could be brought about in local delivery. However, it also inherited from the previous 18 years of Conservative government a commitment to the operations of the economic market and the role of the private sector in the delivery of public services:

> We have rewritten our constitution, the new Clause IV, to put a commitment to enterprise alongside the commitment to justice... Labour offers business a new deal for the future. We will leave intact the main changes of the 1980s in industrial relations and enterprise. We see healthy profits as an essential motor of a dynamic market economy.[62]

Just over ten years later that 'dynamic market economy' is in crisis. There is an overall consensus that the root of the crisis has been in the overgenerous extension of credit to the general public, an extension of credit which was exactly the motor of the dynamism of the economy. Inevitably, there has been political debate as to whether this over-extension occurred over a long period, or was a phenomenon enhanced by the policies of the Labour government post-1997. It can be suggested that even if this latter charge holds good, it was only the case that Labour was simply adapting a basic economic framework taken over from a long period of Conservative rule.

Moving beyond the noise of day-to-day political debate, it is actually more useful in order to analyse the current crisis to turn to Labour's previous period of government in the 1970s. During the *Winter of Discontent*, one of the core questions was the delivery of public services. Kenneth O. Morgan's biography of Prime Minister James Callaghan tells the story in his chapter '*Discontent and decline*':

> From 22nd of January there was even more comprehensive chaos. A million and a half public sector service workers, many of them in NUPE, began haphazard stoppages on behalf of a £60 a week minimum wage. There followed selective stoppages by a variety of public sector workers in hospitals and local government. Sick patients went unattended; schools were closed because of strikes by school caretakers or cooks, or just because they were unheated in freezing weather; ambulance men were failing to answer 999 calls;

---

62   Labour Party Manifesto (1997) *New Labour, because Britain deserves better.*

frozen main roads were not being gritted; dustbin and refuse bags piled up in town centres in their tens of thousands, full of rotting and insanitary waste.[63]

The very infrastructure of public services was perceived by the public to be under threat. This should be set in the context of the contraction of public expenditure triggered by the International Monetary Fund's crisis loan in 1976. The bail-out of the economy had immediate impacts on key areas of public services. The poignant comment of Sir Peter Barclay as Chairman of the National Institute for Social Work, recorded by Nicholas Timmins, is poignant:

> From 1976 on it became a demoralizing fight. Up to that time in social welfare it seemed that all we needed to do was to identify problems, create an organization to cope with them, and that would solve it. Social care, social work, social services – we all had unlimited resources, it then seemed... But from the mid-1970s social services and social care have really been in retreat, certainly beleaguered – more so than social security.[64]

During the 1980s, there was a multifaceted response to all of this. The policy of cuts in public services continued. In part this was owing to economic conditions, but it was also strategic. A workforce with a diminishing number of job openings will tend to be a more disciplined workforce. This reinforced the impact of a whole raft of legislation designed to restrict union rights and the opportunities for industrial disruption. One of the motivators for industrial action had been the making of what were perceived to be inflationary wage demands, as increased wage bills led to price increases, which in turn impelled fresh wage demands. It is here that the extension of credit had its significance. The need was to control the workforce by providing a situation in which *relatively* low paid individuals had access not only to necessary spending but also luxury spending. This kind of spending could be financed by an inflationary wage demand, or secured against the future income of the beneficiary. Increasing generosity of credit ensured the success of legislative initiative and economic strategy in securing a docile workforce. As we have just discovered, generous

---

63   Morgan (1997), p. 663.
64   Timmins (1996), p. 378.

credit cannot be extended indefinitely, secured as it was in this case against a bubble of rising house prices, which eventually burst. The failure of credit imperils the whole structure of control which was the response to the social and economic crisis of the 1970s.

At the time of writing, it is not clear what the way ahead will be. There are number of ideological options. There are those on the right who would argue that the market should be allowed to take its course: that the discipline of the market is the best regulator, and that failing enterprises should be allowed to fail. There is underlying this an attitude to the simple fact of weakness and vulnerability which many of us would find hard to espouse, and even the most right-wing governments – such as that of Bush in the United States – have been prepared to talk of State financial support for the commanding heights of the economy. On other hand, with amazing suddenness some of the economic nostrums of the old left have reappeared, one suspects *faute de mieux*. Alistair Darling has talked of using public sector spending, based on higher levels of public indebtedness, to balance the fall in demand from the private sector during the recession. It is the unexpected return of an old-fashioned Keynesian economics, thought to have become outdated with the rise of Thatcher. It may perhaps be that neither of these options, maintaining capitalism as it is, or fixing capitalism, is going to turn out to be the new discourse.

Writing as I am from the perspective of liberation theology, the old discourse of Marxism has a certain appeal. Adam has a necessarily controlled life, but his life has given me – even if it was not there before – a deep suspicion of systems of control, and certain forms of old Marxism turned out to be nothing but that. So, in place of a large ideology, all I offer is a few suggestions.

We are in that moment when a previous order of things has given way, but its replacement has not yet emerged. We are between the tick and the tock. We need in thought to take ourselves to the time before the economic order of the 1980s established itself, and work our own new response to the circumstances which created that order. Such a response might look something like this:

- We should revisit the 1970s question of public sector pay to ensure that the rewards which our society offers should represent a prioritization of care. Bluntly, it should not be assumed that a career in a caring profession will be relatively badly rewarded: rather we should do what we can to ensure that those who give care in whatever form hold a place of honour within our society.

- Rather than attempting to fix the old, existing economic system, we should be reflecting upon whether it is actually beyond fixing, and that something different, not yet imagined, may emerge to take its place. Money, contract, corporate governance belong to the realms of language, reciprocal socialization and imaginative play. A person with autism can teach us how to step back from those things, and see them from a distance. Adam does not offer a critique of those things; his existence is an unspoken critique of those things. That critique, because it belongs to the realm of the unspoken, to silence, is worked out in spirituality however interpreted. However, if as a society we are having difficulties in the realms of language, socialization and imaginative play, our starting point has to be the recognition and acceptance of ourselves as a fundamentally disabled society.

- Money functions as means of reciprocal exchange because we all accept the rules of the game of exchange, because we imagine the game to work, because we say that the game works. May it be that we are failing to perceive that the actual medium of exchange, our true capital is care given and received?

As a society, we are now at the limits of our understanding of ourselves, at the limits of our technical capacity to resolve the economic and consequent social issues which beset us. It may well be that our lack of capacity to perceive the way ahead for ourselves has brought us to a place of the greatest significance.

CHAPTER 9

The Transformation of the Church

The previous chapter deliberately set alongside each other a range of different kinds of discourse, raising to an acute level the juxtaposition of different kinds of discourse which runs throughout the book. We moved from history, to politics, to theology, sometimes taking some very large leaps upon the way. The last chapter was an experiment to see what happens when those different kinds of discourse are forced into close juxtaposition. This chapter reviews the whole of the book, and examines the consequences – if any – of this text for the life and belief of the Church.

The starting point, in the first chapter, was autism. In creating a theology, the starting point was outside the theological circle. By writing this last chapter, we are taking the movement of the argument into the theological circle. This may be thought of as a pattern for all theological reflection as it forms the life of the Church.

In the second chapter, we examined a life, and indeed lives, lived under extreme circumstances, and – for some of us – under extreme pressure. There is the danger that the Church can become a self-contained form of life, with its own ecclesiastical culture, focused upon internal, sometimes relatively trivial, issues which are not necessarily of interest to the many outside the Church who undergo such extreme experiences. There is here a perhaps rather old-fashioned view that the Church should be relevant, and demonstrate its relevance to such circumstances, a belief that genuine relevance lies at the heart of effective mission.

At the heart of relevance lies an effective response – I do not say answer – to the questions of meaning and purpose set out in the third chapter. Whether they admit it or not, there are many highly reflective and articulate people who experience life as bafflement. This chapter is a plea for the Church that, in attempting to address the questions, does not deny that they exist. Nor should it deny that reality of the experiences which generate such questions.

The question 'why?' arises with particular intensity in a culture shaped by Western individualism: 'why do *I* experience the world in this way?'. The fourth chapter suggests ways in which, in theological and philosophical terms, the energy expended on securing an answer to that question may be better expended in addressing and questioning the roots of the culture within which that question arises. This is not simply a philosophical and theological task. Western individualism is the context in which individual congregations operate. It may well be that one of their primary callings is to hold that culture up to scrutiny, a calling not made easy by the way in which cultural individualism has arisen from the fundamentally individualist nature of the Protestant tradition.

Chapter 5 is a plea for the Church to take the best of modern thought, and to allow its thought to be *fully* formed by that. It is the hope that the Church in that way may maintain its intellectual credibility, be able to participate on an equal footing in what might be rather grandly called the discourses of (post) modernity, without claiming any kind of special privilege for theology, but by insisting also on giving it voice.

Chapters 6 and 7 were located where they are for good reason. Scripture, tradition, liturgy are taken as the foundational bases of the Church, and so they are. Yet they are to be addressed once the preliminary work outlined in the previous chapters has taken place, so that they may be experienced in their full richness. That richness calls for a view of these things that is inclusive: that they may be either accessible or made so. Because they are what they are, simply stopping at making 'reasonable adjustments' is not sufficient: they have to be made accessible to all. Specifically, Bible reading should be done in such way that those with learning disabilities or simple difficulties with handling text are not excluded; the sensuous experience which the best of liturgy is should not be designed simply for those who are the most typical of neurotypicals.

So having done all of this we return to the penultimate chapter. The question down the ages of those who in the dire circumstances in which they found themselves longed for change to take place has been that of agency. Which individual, which group, which class, which party would be the agent of change? 'Who will go for us?' How is the Messiah to be identified? The contention of this book is that the Christian Church, engaged with the bitterness of the day-to-day life of people, engaged with modern thought, engaged and acknowledging the deepest questions of meaning and purpose is called to be – alongside and in community with others – that agent of change.

Yet the Church is not like that. No, it is disabled, not able to do what we might expect of it. And its disability is its glory.

On 28 February 1981, the London *Times* correspondent Clifford Longley reported that the General Synod of the Church of England had held a debate on homosexuality. It should be remembered that when they did so the decriminalization of homosexual activities in the United Kingdom's Sexual Offences Act of 1967 had occurred only 14 years previously, and in one part of the United Kingdom, under the *Criminal Justice (Scotland) Act*, only in the previous year. It was only in 1973 that the the American Psychiatric Association had removed homosexuality from its Diagnostic and Statistical Manual of Mental Disorders (DSM-II).[1] The debate was curtailed when 'the first of a series of motions concerning the moral unacceptability of homosexual behaviour was proposed' and the synod voted to move to next business. Before this happened the then Archbishop of Canterbury, Dr. Robert Runcie had had the opportunity of offering guidance to the Church on how to handle the controversy. Runcie had been a former Guards officer who won a military cross for his wartime bravery. He did not on this occasion reflect the prejudices of his military background, but rather deplored 'the silly insinuations and innuendos, the casual contempt and unthinking mockery of homosexuality which so often passes for discussion of the subject even, alas, in church circles'.

---

1   Now DSM IV – see p. 24 for the use of the DSM in the diagnosis of autism.

'He inclined away' says Longley's report 'from treating homosexuality simply as a sin or a sickness. He preferred to see it as a handicap, a state in which people had to cope with limitations and hardships and in which the fulfilment of heterosexual love and marriage were denied': 'We are learning to treat the handicapped not with pity but with deep respect and an awareness that often through their handicaps they can obtain a degree of self-giving and compassion which are denied to those not similarly afflicted.' But he could not endorse the view that homosexuality 'was a minority but valid alternative to the heterosexual way followed by the majority'.

With the greatest of respect to the late Robert Runcie, I tell this story because it shows the deep connection between the current debates in Anglicanism and some of the themes of this book. The fundamental error is to treat difference as affliction, and to treat those who are different as 'them' rather than 'us'. In them, it is us that we all see.

Epilogue

At the end of *The God Delusion* Richard Dawkins strikes a triumphal note. He wonders if 'by training and practice' we might expand the horizons of our human perception, and thus 'achieve some sort of intuitive – as well as just mathematical understanding of the very small, the very large and the very fast'. He tells us that he 'genuinely' does not know the answer, but that 'I am thrilled to be alive at a time when humanity is pushing against the limits of understanding. Even better, we may eventually discover that there are no limits.'[1] Even in this extreme form, where human replaces divine omniscience, there is much to admire in the great humanist project of the gradual expansion of human understanding. Even in that small segment of the great expanding frontier in which I find myself, there is much to be looked forward to in increasing scientific understanding of autistic spectrum disorders, though with the hope that with understanding will go 'understanding', that as we understand autism, we will stop misunderstanding people with autism, and accept them as they are. However, the experience of living with a person of what is called 'limited' understanding has taught me to understand that there is actually something beyond understanding. To explicate this, I have to turn once more to the earlier work of Wittgenstein. In the *Tractatus Logico-Philosophicus*, Wittgenstein conflates language with scientific language in a way which Dawkins, I suspect, would admire and which Wittgenstein himself seems later to have regretted. Wittgenstein then acknowledges that there are things which do not belong to scientific

---

1   Dawkins (2006), p. 420.

language, which rather belong to silence. At the very end, in a heading all on its own, is the famous statement: 'What we cannot speak about we must pass over in silence.'[2] The exponential increase of human knowledge is not – for me at least – the great narrative. There are certain kinds of things, in and through which we are thrown against incomprehension and misunderstanding. It is in those places that meaning is.

If you the reader have read as far as this, and especially if, as I hope, you have agreed with some things, and disagreed with others, then you and I have been having a conversation. The conversation which I have had with you has been longer, and of a different kind to any conversation which I have ever had with Adam. When I visit Adam, I often talk to him. I can share with him things which I share with few others. When we tell people things we can never be certain beyond mistake that they will not tell others our secrets. I am some-times reluctant to talk to Adam too much. While I want him to hear what language is, so that he can use it in his own way, I do not want to impose upon him the presuppositions of our highly verbal culture. I have disposed elsewhere with the fantasy of 'healing', but that does not prevent me from imagining what I would say to Adam if we could speak together. Similarly, when we receive one of our regular letters from the school, I sometimes ask myself what the letters would look like if I could write back to him, and what the first letter would be...

Dear Adam,

It was good to see you a few weeks ago. I hope you are keeping well. You are now almost as tall as me, and will soon be a man.

I have written a book about you. It is not just about you. It is about God, and philosophers and politicians. When you used to live with us, if you found one of my books, you would tear some of the pages out and try to eat them. I will give you a copy of my book: it is up to you what you do with it. It is not a book about you, it is a book for you.

So, it is actually not my book, but your book. You live in a world that does not allow you to be the author of anything. But it was you who made this book and not me. You are the author of this. Thank you for the words. You have caused some wonderful chaos, but it is a chaos which has proved to be creative.

---

2   Wittgenstein (1961), p.89.

Because our conversation has never begun, it will never end. Other texts end, have a conclusion. I will write again; there is no closure for this. On the day of judgement, no doubt God, or his own Son, will explain autism to me. Until then, I do not think that I understand, I do not think that I will understand.

You are probably one of few Anglican Christians who is not aware that he is an Anglican, or indeed a Christian. Like some of those with autism, you are probably not aware that you are a person with autism, or if you are, you would not call it that.

As Heidegger said, only a God can save us now.

All my love, John.

My conversation with Adam, which this book is, will never be concluded, because never begun. It is the paradigm of the open ended text. St. Mark's Gospel begins with the triumphant announcement of good news: 'The beginning of the Gospel of Jesus Christ, the Son of God.' In some – though not all versions – it ends like this: 'And they (the disciples) said nothing to anybody because they were afraid.' Fear, as far as we know, is not Adam's reason for silence: silence is his way of being, for which he does not need a reason. So to keep all possibilities open, can I ask you the reader to complete, in the words with which you have been gifted: 'Silence is…'?

Afterword

"Humanity is an arriving at, not a departure from"

– Antonio Gramsci

John Gillibrand takes as his starting point the raising of one of his sons, Adam: a young person with severe autism. For most couples, like John and Gillian, parenting is their most stressful adult experience, albeit with occasional very special rewards. As a relative bystander, it is humbling to observe parents' capacity to care, fight and cope over decades. And these are not rare experiences: autism spectrum disorders (ASDs) are common, and extrapolation from prevalence figures in the West suggests that worldwide there may be 62 million people with ASD, similar to the population of the UK. Nevertheless, as with Dawkins' spectrum of religious belief/unbelief, the span of ASDs is great: from individuals such as Adam through to eminent university professors. Indeed, probably only one fifth of people on the spectrum have impaired general intellectual abilities.

But average or superior intelligence is no protection against isolation, marginalization or outright exclusion. Social and communication difficulties and intense or unusual interests can lead to teasing and bullying at school, and although adult peers are usually less hurtful, frequent difficulties finding or maintaining employment, friendships and romantic relationships mean that unremarkable aspirations for a job, house and partner are often not achieved. The human cost of unfulfilled potential is self evident, but governments are usually unaware of the economic costs.

Autism has been the focus of much basic and applied research since its description in the mid 1940s. Initially progress was slow, in part because explanatory models were outdated and in part because the technologies essential for even a partial description of the underlying biology had not yet been invented. Since the mid 1990s there have been significant advances in our understanding of ASDs, mainly because of pressure (and financial support) from parental organizations and technological advances. The capacity to visualize the brain in action, rather than simply to record motor output or speech, is forcing a re-evaluation of the biology underlying the breadth of human behaviour. Imaging research suggests that when able individuals with ASDs achieve normal performance on many different types of tasks, that they do so using a network of brain areas that sometimes is subtly different from what would usually be considered 'normal'. One implication of these findings is that variation in brain mechanisms underlying typical behaviour may be greater than we imagine; marked individual differences may underlie behaviour in the 'normal' range.

Gillibrand notes how civilizations have often marginalized or cloistered those who are different, and very rarely even attempted to eradicate them. It is much easier to promulgate inclusion than to achieve it. Whilst there is a role for legislation, its utility is limited in the context of ignorance. The family next door, teachers, peers, work colleagues will usually struggle to accept what they do not grasp. The challenge is to educate citizens to understand why individuals with ASD behave in the way that they sometimes do; once we understand we broaden the scale against which we judge, and autistic behaviour can be encompassed within our concept of humanity. Do unto others as you would have them do unto you.[1]

Anthony Bailey
Professor of Child and Adolescent Psychiatry,
University of British Columbia,
February 2010

---

1   Matthew 7:12; Matthew 22:39.

Sources of Help

Some of those reading this book will have been directly affected by the issues discussed. It is on occasions most important to seek and to obtain help and assistance.

The National Autistic Society
393 City Road, London, EC1V 1NG
www.nas.org.uk
+44 (0)20 7833 2299 HELPLINE: 0845 070 4004
The National Autistic Society maintains the *Autism Services Directory* which can be found at: http://www.autismdirectory.org.uk

Autism Speaks (UK)
North Lea House, 66 Northfield End, Henley-on-Thames, Oxfordshire, RG9 2BE
http://www.autismspeaks.org.uk
+44 (0)1491 412311

Autism Speaks (USA)
2 Park Avenue, 11th Floor, New York, NY 10016
http://www.autismspeaks.org
(212) 252-8584

Autism Society of America
7910 Woodmont Avenue, Suite 300, Bethesda, Maryland 20814-3067
http://www.autism-society.org
(301) 657-0881
Information on different types of local services in the USA can be found at: http://www.autismsource.org/

Autism NI (PAPA)
Donard, Knockbracken Healthcare Park, Saintfield Road, Belfast, BT8 8BH

Scottish Society for Autism
Hilton House, Alloa Business Park, Whins Road, Alloa, FK10 3SA
http://www.autism-in-scotland.org.uk
+44 (0)1259 720044

Autism Cymru
6 Great Darkgate Street, Aberystwyth, SY23 1DE
http://www.awares.org
+44(0)1970 625256.

Irish Society for Autism
Unity Building, 16/17 Lower O'Connell Street, Dublin, 1
www.autism.ie
01 8744684

Irish Autism Action
41 Newlands, Mullingar, Co. Westmeath.
http://www.autismireland.ie
044-9331609
NATIONAL AUTISM HELPLINE: 1890 818 518

Bibliography

Aarons, M. and Gittens, T. (1992) *The Handbook of Autism – a guide for parents and professionals.* London and New York: Routledge.

Adams, M,M. and Adams, R.M. (eds.) (1990) *The Problem of Evil (Oxford Readings in Philosophy).* Oxford: Oxford University Press.

All-party Parliamentary Group on Mental Health (2008) *Mental Health in Parliament.* http://www.mind.org.uk/News+policy+and+campaigns/Press/2008-07-16-APPGMH.htm [accessed 29 July 2008].

Augustine (ed. Knowles, D., trans. Bettenson, H.) (1972) *The City of God.* London: Penguin.

Avalos, H., Melcher, S.J., Schipper, J. (eds.) (2007) *This Abled Body: rethinking disabilities and biblical studies.* Atlanta: Society of Biblical Literature.

Bagchi, D. and Steinmetz, D.C. (eds.) (2004) *The Cambridge Companion to Reformation Theology.* Cambridge: Cambridge University Press.

Baron-Cohen, S. (1995) *Mindblindness – an essay on autism and theory of mind.* Massachusetts: MIT Press.

Baron-Cohen, S., Tager-Flusberg, H., Cohen, D.J. (eds.) (1993) *Understanding Other Minds – perspectives from autism (Oxford Medical Publications).* Oxford: Oxford University Press.

Bogdashina, O. (2003) *Sensory and Perceptual Issues in Autism and Asperger Syndrome – different sensory experiences, different perceptual worlds.* London and Philadelphia: Jessica Kingsley Publishers.

Borsay, A. (2005) *Disability and Social Policy in Britain Since 1750 – a history of exclusion.* London: Palgrave Macmillan.

Burckhardt, J. (trans. Middlemore, S.G.C.) (1990) *The Civilisation of the Renaissance in Italy.* London: Penguin.

Burke, S. (1995) *Authorship: from Plato to the postmodern. A reader.* Edinburgh: Edinburgh University Press.

Cameron, D. (ed.) (1990) *The Feminist Critique of Language.* London: Routledge.

Carr, A. *The Handbook of Child and Adolescent Psychology – a contextual approach.* London and New York: Routledge.

Commission for Social Care Inspection (2008) *The State of Social Care in England 2006–7: CSCI's Third Annual Report to Parliament on the State of Social Care.* Presented to Parliament under section 129 (1)(b) of the Health and Social Care (Community Health and Standards) Act 2003.

Cottingham, J. (ed.) (1992) *Cambridge Companion to Descartes.* Cambridge: Cambridge University Press.

Davies, O. and Turner, D. (eds) (2002) *Silence and the Word – negative theology and incarnation.* Cambridge: Cambridge University Press.

Davis, L.J. (ed.) (1997) *The Disability Studies Reader.* London and New York: Routledge.

Dawkins, R. (2006) *The God Delusion.* London: Transworld.

De Beauvoir, S. (1965, trans. Green, P.) *The Prime of Life.* London: Penguin.

Department of Health (2001) Valuing People: A New Strategy for Learning Disability for the 21st Century. A White Paper. http://www.archive.official-documents.co.uk/document/cm50/5086/5086.pdf [accessed 8 February, 2010]

Derrida, J. (1972, ed. 1981) *Dissemination.* London/New York: Continuum.

Derrida, J. (1994, ed. 2006) *Specters of Marx – the state of the debt, the work of mourning and the New International.* London: Routledge (in the Routledge Classics series).

Descartes, R. (1968, trans. Sutcliffe, F.E.) *Discourse on Method* and *The Meditations.* London: Penguin.

Eiesland, N. L. (1994) *The Disabled God – toward a liberatory theology of disability.* Nashville: Abingdon Press.

Feldman, D. (2002) *Civil Liberties and Human Rights in England and Wales.* Oxford: Oxford University Press.

Foucault, M. (1966) *Les Mots et les Choses.* Paris: Gallimard.

Foucault, M. (ed. and intro. Kritzman, L.D.) (1988) *Michel Foucault – politics, philosophy, culture. Interviews and other writings. 1977–1984.* London: Routledge.

Fredman, S. (2008) *Human Rights Transformed – positive rights and positive duties.* Oxford: Oxford University Press.

Frith, U. (1989, 2nd ed. 2003) *Autism, explaining the enigma.* Oxford: Blackwell.

Gutiérrez, G. (1987 translation) *On Job – God-talk and the suffering of the innocent.* New York: Orbis.

Gutiérrez, G. (2001) *A Theology of Liberation.* London: SCM.

Gutting, G. (2001) *French Philosophy in the Twentieth Century.* Cambridge: Cambridge University Press.

Happé, F. (1994) *Autism – an introduction to psychological theory.* London: UCL Press.

Hick, J. (1966, 1977, 1985) *Evil and the God of Love.* London: Macmillan.

Hick, J. (ed.) (1964) *The Existence of God* (in the Problems of Philosophy series). London: Macmillan.

Hopkins, Gerard Manley (ed.) (1953) *Poems and Prose – selected and edited by W.H. Gardner.* London: Penguin.

Horsman, S. (1989) *Living With Stress – a guide for ministers and church leaders.* Cambridge: Lutterworth Press.

Houston, R. and Frith, U. (2000) *Autism in History – the case of Hugh Blair of Borgue.* Oxford: Blackwell.

Hull, J.M. (2001) *In the Beginning There was Darkness.* London: SCM.

Jones, C., Wainright, G. Yarnold, E. (eds.) (1978, eighth impression 1987) *The Study of Liturgy.* London: SPCK.

Kershaw, I. (2000) *Hitler 1936–1945: Nemesis.* London: Penguin.

Kraut, R. (ed.) (1992) *The Cambridge Companion to Plato*. Cambridge: Cambridge University Press.

Lang. C.G. (1900) *The Miracles of Jesus as Marks the Way of Life*. London: Isbister and Company.

MacCulloch, D. (2003) *Reformation – Europe's house divided 1490–1700*. London: Penguin.

Mandelstam, M. (2005) *Community Care Practice and the Law* (third edition). London: Jessica Kingsley Publishers.

Matarasso, P. (ed. and trans.) (1993) *The Cistercian World – monastic writings of the twelfth century*. London: Penguin.

McNay, L. (1994) *Foucault – a critical introduction*. Cambridge: Polity Press.

Merleau-Ponty, M. (trans. C. Smith) (2002) *Phenomenlogy of Perception*. London: Routledge.

Michael, J. (2008) *Healthcare for All – Independent inquiry into access to healthcare for people with learning disabilities.* http://www.dh.gov.uk/prod_consum_dh/groups/dh_digitalassets/@dh/@en/documents/digitalasset/dh_106126.pdf [accessed on 5 January 2010]

Moltmann, J. (1985) *God in Creation – an ecological doctrine of creation* (The Gifford Lectures 1984–1985). London: SCM Press.

Moltmann, J. (2000) *Experiences in Theology – ways and forms of Christian theology*. London: SPCK.

Moran, D. (2000) *Introduction to Phenomenology*. London and New York: Routledge.

Morgan, H. (1996) *Adults with Autism – a guide to theory and practice*. Cambridge: Cambridge University Press.

Morgan, K.O. (1997) *Callaghan – A Life*. Oxford: Oxford University Press.

Moss, J. (ed.) (1998) *The Later Foucault*. London: Sage.

Osbourne, L.A. and Reed, P. (2008) 'Parents' perceptions of communication with professionals during the diagnosis of autism.' *Autism* vol. 12, no. 3, May.

Porter, R. (1987, new ed. Tempus 2006) *Madmen – a social history of madhouses, mad-doctors and lunatics*. Stroud: Tempus. Originally published by Athlone Press as *Mind Forg'd Manacles*.

Ramsey, M. (1972, rev. ed. 1987) *The Christian Priest Today*. London: SPCK.

Read, J. and Clements, L. (2001) *Disabled Children and the Law – research and good practice*. London: Jessica Kingsley Publishers.

Robinson, V. G. (2008) *In the Eye of the Storm*. Norwich: Canterbury Press.

Rolle. R. (trans. Wolters, C.) (1972) *The Fire of Love*. London: Penguin.

Schacht, R. (ed.) (1993) *Nietzsche – selections* [in the Great Philosophers series]. New York: Macmillan.

Sear, C. (2005) *Electoral Franchise: Who can vote?* London: House of Commons Library.

Swinburne, R. (1977, rev. ed. 1993) *The Coherence of Theism* (Clarendon Library of Logic and Philosophy). Oxford: Clarendon Press.

Swinton, J. (ed.) (2004) *Critical Reflections on Stanley Hauerwas' Theology of Disability*. New York: Haworth Pastoral Press.

Tillich, P. (ed.) (1978) *Systematic Theology, volume 2*. London: SCM. First published in 1957.

Timmins, N. (1996) *The Five Giants: A Biography of the Welfare State*. London: Fontana.

Tremain, S. (ed.) (2005) *Foucault and the Government of Disability*. Ann Arbor: University of Michigan Press.

Vanier, J. (1979, 3rd revised edition, 2007) *Community and Growth.* London: Darton. Longman, Todd.

Williams, M.L. (2007) *Beauty and Brokeness: compassion and the Kingdom of God.* London: SPCK.

Williams, R. (2000) *On Christian Theology.* Oxford: Blackwell.

Wing, L. (1996) *The Autistic Spectrum: a guide for parents and professionals.* London: Constable.

Wittgenstein, L. (1951, 3rd ed. 2001) *Philosophical Investigations – the German text with a revised English Translation.* Oxford: Blackwell.

Wittgenstein, L. (1961, revised edition 1974) *Tractatus Logico-Philosophicus.* London: RKP.

Wood, D. (ed.) (1992) *Derrida – a critical reader.* Oxford: Blackwell.

Woodruff Smith, D. (2007) *Husserl.* London and New York: Routledge.

Young, F. (1990, further impression 1998) *Face to Face – a narrative essay in the theology of suffering.* Edinburgh: T & T Clark.

The Book of Common Prayer for Use in the Church in Wales (1984) Cardiff: Church in Wales Publications.

Valuing People: A New Strategy for Learning Disability for the 21st Century (2001) London: HMSO.

Subject Index

Author Index